MAKING
WOODEN TOYS
FOR ALL AGES

MAKING
WOODEN TOYS
FOR ALL AGES

Bryan Mapstone

A DAVID & CHARLES CRAFT BOOK

DEDICATION

This book is dedicated to my wife Susan for her support
during its writing, and to my children Peter, Gemma, Rachel
and Alison who enjoyed being my unpaid official testers.

British Library Cataloguing in Publication Data
Mapstone, Bryan
  Making wooden toys for all ages.
  1. Wooden toys. Making. Manuals
  I. Title
  745.592

  ISBN 0-7153-9382-0 (H/b)
  ISBN 0-7153-9809-1 (P/b)

  © text and line drawings: Bryan Mapstone 1989
  © colour photographs: David & Charles plc 1989

Phototypeset by Typesetters (Birmingham) Ltd
and printed in Great Britain
by Redwood Burn Ltd, Trowbridge
for David & Charles Publishers plc
Brunel House   Newton Abbot   Devon

Distributed in the United States by
Sterling Publishing Co, Inc,
2 Park Avenue, New York NY 10016

CONTENTS

INTRODUCTION

Whether you are experienced at DIY or not, *Making Wooden Toys For All Ages* contains something for everyone. There are projects within this book to keep both the beginner and the experienced crafts-man happy for many hours, and the children for even longer.

The initial cost of this book will be recouped as soon as you have completed your first project. You will not only be able to save money by making toys for your own children, but by making them for relatives and friends' children as well.

Lots of helpful hints are included to make life easier for the beginner, and the accomplished woodworker will also benefit as he or she will not have to spend time working out plans. Work can begin as soon as the book is opened.

If you are a beginner and do not have a fully equipped workshop, work can be carried out on a portable workmate with equally good results.

Unlike the mass-produced, and often expensive, toys on sale in the shops, your finished wooden toy will bear its own individual mark. Children do realise and understand the time and effort a person has put into building and painting their present. All of my children are very proud of the toys I design and produce for them. They are now even taking an interest in the actual making of the toys, and are giving me so many ideas that I can't keep up with them all.

All the toys in this book have been designed with strength and safety in mind and you can rest assured that your child will come to no harm playing with the toys you have made.

UNDERSTANDING THE DRAWINGS

The first step to making any of the projects in this book is to understand the drawings. Each dimension contains two sets of figures, eg 102(4). The number 102 represents millimetres (metric), the number (4) in the brackets represents inches (imperial). Very often the metric number may not be an exact equivalent of the imperial number. Whichever system you choose to use, stick to it throughout. Using the metric system is not as difficult as might at first be thought; with practice, you will probably find it easier to work with than all those fractions of inches.

There are six different types of lines used on the drawings which may be confusing if you have never seen a mechanical drawing before. A brief description of the meaning of each line follows with a simple example:

1 *Continuous (thick)*
These denote the outline of a component that *can* be seen from the direction the drawing is viewed, eg Cottage Night Light (Fig 2).
2 *Continuous (thin)*
These are dimension lines, eg Cottage Night Light (Fig 1).
3 *Short dashes (thin)*
These denote the outline of an area or component that *can not* be seen from the direction the drawing is viewed, because it is obscured by one or more parts. These lines then refer to hidden detail, eg Cottage Night Light (Fig 3).
4 *Long dashes (thin)*
These denote the outline position of a named component which is to be fitted in the position shown at a later stage of construction, eg Rescue Centre (Fig 1).
5 *Dashes broken by a dot*
These denote the centre line between two points or edges, eg Cottage Night Light (Fig 1).
6 *Section lining (hatching)*
Thin parallel lines drawn at an angle of 45°. These denote the part of a component which remains after a portion is assumed to have been cut away and/or removed.

Terms and Abbreviations
used on drawings and cutting lists

dia	–	diameter
csk	–	countersink
mm	–	millimetres
in	–	inches
rad	–	radius
lh	–	left-hand
rh	–	right-hand
pitch	–	fixing angle of a component
ancillaries	–	non-wooden components

METHODS AND MATERIALS

Cutting lists

Each project includes a complete list of parts, their relevant sizes and materials required to make them. Used in conjunction with the drawings, you will find the cutting lists very useful for keeping track of parts as you make them.

Materials

Many projects in this book require plywood for some, or all, of their construction. Birch plywood should be used for these parts because it is safer for children. It has a tighter grain and more laminations than ordinary plywood, therefore making it stronger. It does not readily tear when it is sawn or knocked, and it is better suited all round to the rigours of child play. It is more expensive than ordinary plywood but, because of its higher quality, it is well worth the extra expense. Painting, varnishing and rubbing down are a lot easier as there is no grain filling to be done and a perfect finish can be achieved every time. For most of the projects, soft wood will be sufficient, but to obtain the best results when making the Spirit of America Wrecker Truck (page 112), the Off-road Racer (page 70), the Four-wheel-drive Vehicle (page 74) and Trailer (page 85), hardwood should be used.

All dimensions given for wood are finished sizes. When ordering wood, it is important to stress this to your supplier.

Working with metal

Metal parts are used on certain projects where strength and minimum thickness of material are required. Stainless steel should be used for these parts because of its strength, bright appearance and resistance to corrosion.

Tools required for working with metal are: files, scriber, felt-tip pen, hacksaw (large), centre punch, twist drills for metal cutting. When marking out metal parts, draw a rough outline of the part required onto the metal using a large felt-tip pen allowing the ink to dry. Then, mark onto the metal the exact shape required using a metal scriber or compass point. Using this method of marking out, cutting lines will be clearly visible.

Use a centre punch or nail point to mark hole centres; drills will wander if this is not done, resulting in inaccurately drilled holes. When working with metal you must ensure that the edges of all metal parts are filed off, and that they are smooth to the touch. Alway hold metal parts to be worked securely in a vice, or with hand-held vice grips, etc. If parts are not held securely, especially when drilling, the drill bit could catch in the metal which will spin around, resulting in possible serious injury to you, or a bystander. Remove any scratches from your metal workpiece with 1200-grade wet and dry abrasive paper used wet, and finally polish them with metal polish.

Marking out

This is the first stage in any construction and it is where mistakes can easily happen. A sharp trimming or marking knife is ideal for marking across wood grain because it will make a thin, easy-to-follow line, cutting the fibres of the wood which reduces the chances of the wood tearing when it is cut. Use a hard pencil when marking with the grain, and to shade areas that have to be removed when cutting out slots, tags, windows, etc. Without this shading it is quite easy to remove the wrong area. This is both wasteful and time consuming.

Cutting out

Whether you use an electrical jigsaw or a hand saw to cut out your pieces, always secure your work firmly in a vice or to a bench or table with the appropriate cramps. When cutting plywood with an electric jigsaw, always use a fine blade; this will reduce splitting. Always cut on the waste side of a line.

Window, door and slot openings

These are achieved by drilling two holes (which are large enough to accept your saw blade) in diagonal corners of the window, door, etc to be removed. Insert a coping saw (jigsaw) blade into one of these holes, and cut to both of its adjacent corners. Remove the saw blade and insert it into the remaining hole; repeat the process. A file can then be used to smooth the edges of the opening. As a safety measure, always put handles on files.

Sharpening chisels, etc
Sharp tools are a must when working with wood, and time spent sharpening them will be well rewarded. If you find it difficult to sharpen tools, honing guides are available in most DIY shops that will help you get a perfect cutting edge every time. Use an oil stone to sharpen tools. Remember – blunt tools are dangerous.

Countersinking
This is a method of getting a screw head below or flush with the material it is screwed into. A drill bit the same diameter as the screw head can be used for this purpose, although an inexpensive countersink bit is preferable.

Cup washers
These are sometimes used underneath screw heads when the screw head is visible and in a prominent position. Cup washers will give a more pleasing appearance to the finish of a project than countersunk screw heads and are available in either brass or bright zinc finishes (see the Spirit of America Wrecker Truck, colour photo page 129).

Pilot holes
These are small holes which allow the insertion of a screw without splitting the surrounding material. They are essential when screwing into hard wood. A pilot hole should be drilled smaller than the thread size of the screw used.

Wheels
Model and craft magazines usually carry adverts from suppliers of most craft ancillaries (including wheels) and these can invariably be bought by mail order.

Spring hub caps
These are used to keep axles and other shafts etc in position. To fit them, gently tap them onto a shaft with a hammer. Hold each hub cap in position and protect it as it is being fitted by placing a piece of PVC insulation tape over it.

Adhesives
Adhesives (glues) are available for a multitude of specific uses, and it is important that the correct adhesive is used for the job in hand. For the majority of projects throughout this book, use waterproof wood adhesive. Use adhesive sparingly, and wipe away any excess with a damp cloth before it has dried. Contact adhesives should be avoided when bonding wood to wood, eg joints, because they are still flexible when dry.

Finishing off
Before any painting is attempted, use a fine grade abrasive paper to rub down your projects. Make sure that all edges are also smoothed off to reduce the risk of them splitting or tearing when in use. Remove all dust from your project by using a cloth which has been damped with white spirit or turpentine substitute. After every coat of paint or varnish (except the final coat) lightly rub down your project with fine abrasive paper and try and store it away from any dust while the paint or varnish is drying. If the project is small enough, a cardboard box can be placed over it. Only paint and fillers which are safe for children to handle should be used, ie lead-free paint.

The drying time of paint or varnish is very dependent on temperature, and if you are painting your projects in a shed or garage during the winter months it is a good idea to bring them into the home overnight to allow them to dry properly.

A bad construction can be covered up with a good paint job, but a good construction can be ruined with a bad paint job. Don't be surprised if putting the finishing touches to your project takes longer than its construction. Any time spent on finishing is well worth the extra effort.

Dry rub-on lettering can be used to improve a project, and use of an indelible marker pen can also add realism and character if lining is required.

HAND TOOLS:
THEIR USES AND SAFETY

Although a lot of jobs these days are done with machines and computers, there is still a place for hand tools. They can be used anywhere and are obviously not affected by electrical power cuts. Choosing hand tools must be given careful consideration, and buying a reputable brand of tool will pay dividends in the long run. A cheap tool may look identical to a more expensive one, but the difference will be in the quality of materials used in its construction and the method of manufacture, not just the brand name.

The following descriptions, uses and drawings of hand tools were compiled with the help of Stanley Tools and Record Marples Tools. If you require any further information and/or help in choosing hand tools, Stanley Tools have prepared 36 fact sheets (to date) which are available free from some tool outlets. Or consult a tool catalogue, which should also be free.

Tenon or back saw
Produces light accurate straight cuts either along or across a piece of wood, eg general bench work and cutting joints. The back keeps the blade rigid and may be made of brass or steel. Brass is generally found on top-quality saws.

Hand saw
Produces long straight cuts either along or across a piece of wood, eg cutting boards and sheet materials to size.

Chisels (1)
For general DIY use around the house you will need a minimum of three chisels: 6mm (¼in); 12mm (½in); and 25mm (1in). Later, other sizes can be added. The firmer bevel edge chisel is the most versatile pattern. A chisel's main use is for removing waste wood. This can be to form a joint, or simply to shape the corner of a piece of wood.

Spokeshave
A spokeshave will enable you to shape curved surfaces both concave and convex as there are two types available; one having a flat sole and one curved.

Bench plane (2)
This is a tool which basically holds a 'chisel' type of blade firmly to make a controlled and accurate cut or shaving. This is achieved by allowing the blade to protrude very slightly through the sole of the plane, and the depth of cut adjustment and lateral adjusting lever control this. There is a great variety of types and sizes of planes available, and some are for specialised tasks, eg cutting grooves, rebates or convex and concave curves.

In general, a smoothing plane with a sole length of 245mm (9¾in) and a cutter width of 50mm (2in) will be a good start to your tool kit.

Honing guide
This is a very useful accessory which will help you sharpen chisels and plane blades to their correct angle.

Marking gauge (3)
Used for marking lines parallel to an edge with the grain.

Mortise gauge
Used for accurately marking out both mortises and tenons so that they are both the same.

G cramp (4)
These come in varying sizes and can be used for a variety of clamping jobs such as securing a piece of work to a bench or table, or securing two or more pieces of wood together while the glue is allowed to harden.

Sash cramps
These are primarily designed for the cramping of large sections of work during joint glueing. With the addition of lengthening bars their capacity can be increased.

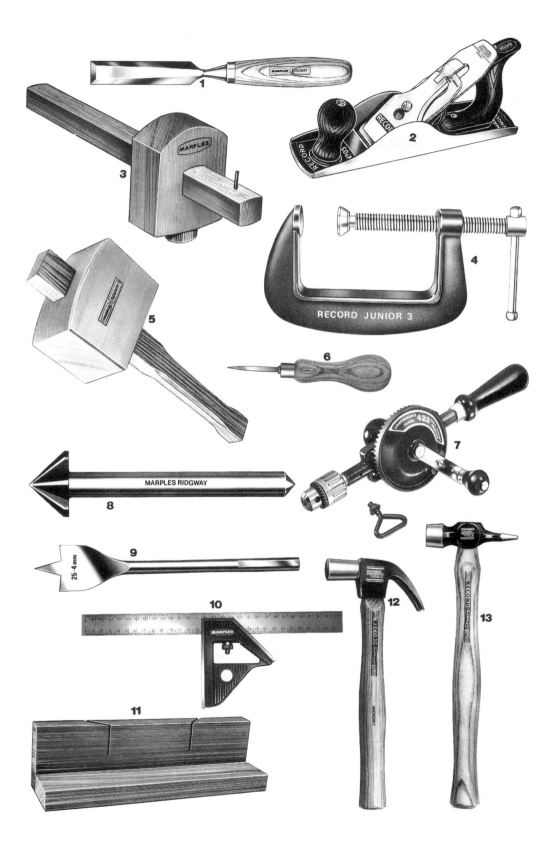

Woodworker's bench vice
Available in varying sizes and costs, they are as invaluable to the amateur as they are to the professional. Some vices are fitted with a very useful quick release mechanism.

Joiner's mallet (**5**)
Should be used for chiselling and assembly operations in preference to a steel hammer so that damage does not occur to your chisel or work piece.

Bradawl (**6**)
For starting screw holes to prevent splitting the wood.

Hand drill (**7**)
Used for accurate drilling of small diameter holes.

Countersink bit (**8**)
To enable a screw head to sit flush with the surface of the wood, screw holes must be countersunk using this special bit.

Flat bit (**9**)
Designed specifically for use with an electrical drill it bores holes quickly, cleanly and safely in all types of wood and many other materials. A minimum drill speed of 1,000 rpm should be used, and all size flat bits work efficiently at 2,500 rpm.

To use a flat bit, drill partly through your workpiece from one side until the tip of the bit starts to appear on the reverse side. Remove the bit; insert it into the small hole made on the reverse side and finish drilling hole.

Combination square (**10**)
An all-purpose square it will mark out both 90° and 45° angles. The sliding head can be locked in any position to check surfaces and angles. It can also be used as a rule.

Sliding bevel
This is a try-square which can be adjusted and locked to any angle for marking angles or checking angular surfaces.

Mitre block/box (**11**)
Both of these are used as a saw guide for cutting angles of 45° and 90°.

Bench hook
For helping to secure wood when sawing with a tenon or back saw at 90°.

Claw hammer (**12**)
Ideal for heavy nailing jobs and the removal of old nails.

Warrington hammer (**13**)
Suitable for light joinery work, ie picture framing, fixing wallboards to battens, securing hardboard/plywood etc.

Trimming knife
There are many different types of this knife available, and which to choose is a matter of personal preference, but one that has a retractable blade should be considered for safety reasons. Uses of these knives are too numerous and varied to list, but they are very useful when marking cross grain lines because they cut the wood's fibres cleanly and finely. If fitted with a small saw blade, the knife will double up as a keyhole saw.

Flexible steel tape measure
These are available in different lengths and will measure both metric and imperial. Most blades are replaceable to increase the life of the rule. Do *not* use these rules for marking straight lines.

Workmate
For people who do not have access to permanently erected benches in a garage or shed, a workmate is the ideal solution when looking for a mobile work station. Work can be carried out anywhere around the house and the workmate can then be folded away. The top of the workmate opens and closes just like a vice, and so work pieces can be held firmly in position.

Hand tools safety check list
It is not only power tools that are a potential danger to their users. Hand tools if not used correctly can also be dangerous. Always ask advice from your tool supplier if you are not sure of something, or visit your local library for a book dealing specifically with the use of tools.

Below is a short list of safety hints which you may find helpful.

Never
1 Never use a tool for any purpose other than that for which it is designed.
2 Never use the side of a hammer to strike metal objects.
3 Never use a hammer which has a dirty face as it will tend to slip.
4 Never use tools that are broken or damaged. Repair properly or replace them.
5 Never push metal objects in the mouth of a plane to release jammed shavings.
6 Never use a flexible steel tape measure as a guide when marking with a sharp trimming knife.
7 Never stand a plane upright as damage to the blade may occur.
8 Never test the sharpness of any blade, chisel, etc by applying direct pressure to the edge with fingers or thumb.

Always
1 Always use sharp chisels, planes, etc. Blunt tools require more effort for them to cut, and are therefore less controllable.
2 Always, when using any type of saw, start your cut slowly using your thumb nail as a guide. When the saw cut has started, move your steadying hand well clear of the blade in case it jumps out.
3 Always use a solid straight-edge when marking with a trimming knife.
4 Always secure your work firmly to a bench, table or vice before carrying out any work on it.
5 Always keep tools out of reach of children.
6 Always ensure that your work area is clean and tidy.

POWER TOOLS:
THEIR USES AND SAFETY

Power tools are a great aid to have in a home workshop. Experience in their use has to be learnt as with hand tools, but when this experience has been gained, power tools will help you carry out lots of jobs in and around the home more quickly and easily.

Choosing a power tool to suit a particular need can be difficult for both the beginner and the more experienced craftsman alike. Your local dealer should be able to help you make the choice that is right for you.

There are two main categories of power tools available, DIY and professional. DIY tools have been developed for the occasional home user and are more than adequate for this purpose. Professional tools are designed for continuous and more rigorous everyday uses in various professions. Because of this, professional quality tools are usually more expensive than DIY tools.

Linking these two main categories however, is the Black & Decker Power Plus range. This range of tools combines qualities that are found in both DIY and professional tools at a reasonable cost. When you have decided how much work you are going to have for a particular tool, this will then dictate the class of tool to be purchased, ie DIY, Power Plus or professional.

The following drawings, descriptions and uses of power tools have been compiled with the help of Black & Decker Power Tools Ltd and are only intended to be a brief guide. If any further information is required, this should be available from a power tool stockist.

Electric drill (1)
This is probably the most widely used of all power tools. Electronic speed control which is available on some models will enable you to drill most materials and

start drilling at slower speeds for greater accuracy.

Vertical drill stand

Where accuracy is essential in drilling holes at exactly 90° to the horizontal, a vertical drill stand is indispensable. By using the drill stand's depth gauge, fine adjustments can be achieved for exact drilling depth. A machine vice can also be fitted which will help when drilling small, round or metal objects.

Jigsaw (2)

By changing the speed of a jigsaw (electronic only), and using different blades to suit the material to be cut, the jigsaw can be a very useful and versatile tool. The 'sole' of a jigsaw can be adjusted so that it will cut angles between 45° and 90°. An electronic pendulum jigsaw, sometimes called an orbital jigsaw which has a dust-blower and plunger safety guard, is ideally suited to most work you will ever have to do. Jigsaws cut on the up stroke and this can sometimes result in damage to the material being cut. To avoid this damage showing, mark and cut your work piece on its reverse side.

Planing machine (3)

A planing machine will enable you to turn a rough piece of waste wood into a smooth re-usable work piece with the minimum of fuss. Used inverted with a bench support and blade guard, the planing machine can be operated for stationary work and small work pieces. By setting the depth gauge and using a parallel guide, rebates can also be cut.

Orbital sander (4)

Generally used for finishing work. By adjusting the speed of an electronic orbital sander and using different grade abrasive papers, it is possible to use it for sanding materials such as heat sensitive plastic, and for removing old paint from woodwork.

Belt sander

Generally these are used for heavy duty sanding. If inverted and bench mounted, a belt sander can be very successfully

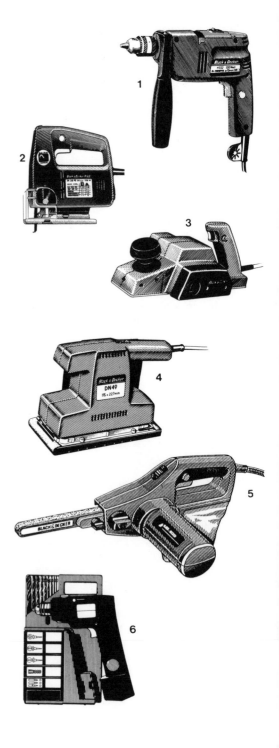

used for sharpening tools and more importantly to sand and shape work pieces.

Power file (5)

The power file is a recent addition to the family of power tools, and its uses are many and varied. As with most power tools, the power file is available either as a standard model or a variable speed electronic model which will give greater versatility to the user. The power file is very useful when making openings (windows, etc), smoothing end grain, slot cutting or shaping bulky items such as the Off-road Racer (page 70). With a special attachment it can also be used bench mounted as a mini belt sander for shaping materials or sharpening tools.

Cordless drill/screwdriver (6)

Cordless battery power gives you the chance to do DIY tasks in places you could never reach with conventional power tools. There are no restricting power cables to snag or trip over which makes life that little bit easier when working in confined spaces such as a shed or small workroom. Because of their slow speed cordless drills are excellent for screwdriving, and also stirring paint. The recharge time of cordless tools can vary, but an average time is approximately 1 hour.

Power tools safety check list

Most accidents that happen to people using power tools occur in and around the home, and so care must be taken when using them to minimise any potential danger. If you have any worries about using power tools, most tool dealers will provide helpful assistance and possibly a demonstration.

Never

1 Never carry a power tool around if it is switched on and running.
2 Never wear loose clothing or ties while operating power tools.
3 Never make adjustments to power tools while they are plugged in.
4 Never leave a power tool plugged in and unattended, especially if children are present.
5 Never use accessories which are not designed for your power tool.
6 Never use a power tool for any purpose other than that for which it is designed.

Always

1 Always read the manufacturer's literature before operating an unfamiliar power tool.
2 Always ensure that the floor area you are working in is clean and tidy.
3 Always wear sound footwear.
4 If your machine has a lock ON switch, always make sure it is in the OFF position before plugging it in.
5 If you have long hair, always tie it up out of the way or cover it up.
6 Always keep power cables free from obstruction and saw blades etc. If a power tool is continually used for bench work, chaffing can occur on the power cable so check this regularly.
7 When using accessories, always ensure they are right for your machine and that they are fitted and adjusted correctly.
8 Always wear protective clothing etc where appropriate; eg safety goggles and dust mask.

DOLL'S ROCKING CRADLE

Cradles of similar design to this one have been rocking babies to sleep and keeping them snug and warm for hundreds of years. Although this cradle is made from modern birch plywood, it has been finished with a deep mahogany stain gloss varnish to compliment the traditional design.

It must be stressed that this cradle is designed *specifically for dolls* and is too small for real babies.

1 As will be seen from the drawings, there are two large radii, 423mm (16⅝in) and 204mm (8in). These are probably outside the scope of any compass you may have at home, and so you will have to make one. Simply take a batten of wood with a minimum length of 459mm (18⅛in), drive a nail into one end to form the compass point, and drill two holes (pencil size) the correct distances (see above) away from the nail point for the insertion of a pencil to draw the arcs.

2 With the aid of your new 'jumbo' compass, mark and cut out one end panel (Fig 1), drilling four 4mm (³⁄₁₆in) dia holes as shown.

Fig 1 End panel
make two, 12 (½) thick

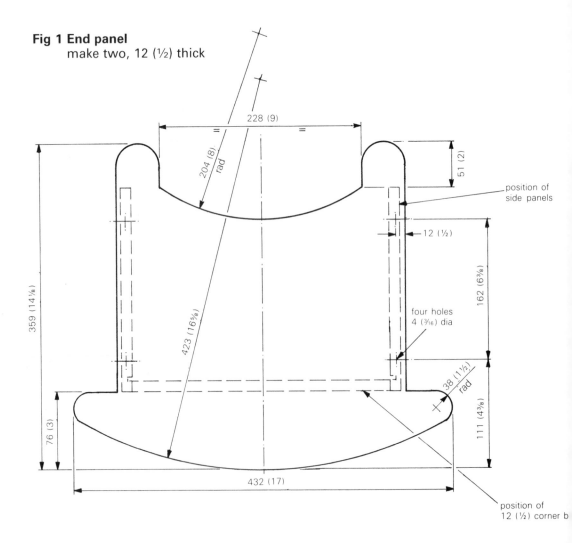

Fig 2 Side panel
make two, 12 (½) thick

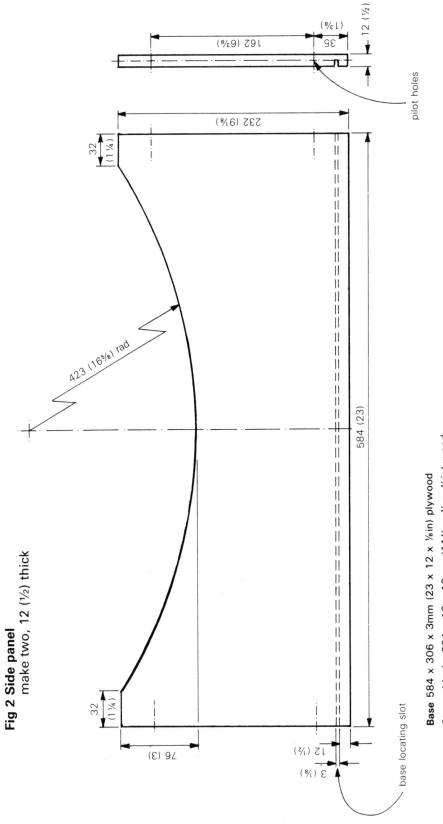

162 (6⅜)   35   12 (½)
(1⅜)

pilot holes

232 (9⅛)

32 (1¼)

423 (16⅝) rad

584 (23)

32 (1¼)

76 (3)

12 (½)

3 (⅛)

base locating slot

Base 584 x 306 x 3mm (23 x 12 x ⅛in) plywood

Corner blocks 294 x 12 x 12mm (11½ x ½ x ½in) wood

3 Use the end panel (Fig 1) you have just cut out as a template to mark out the remaining end panel, which is then cut out and drilled.

4 Again using the 'jumbo' compass, mark and cut out one side panel (Fig 2). As with the end panels, the first side panel to be cut out will serve as a pattern for the marking out of the second. When both side panels have been cut out, drill two pilot holes in each end as shown. These pilot holes will ensure accurate alignment when assembling.

5 To mark out the heart shape on each side panel, draw a full-size grid in the required position and transpose the heart (Fig 3) one square at a time.

6 A groove is cut into each side panel to secure the base and keep its edges out of sight. If however, you do not have the equipment to cut the groove, all is not lost. Simply make the base 12mm (½in) wider than specified in the cutting list and screw directly to the underside of each side face.

7 To assemble, glue the base into the grooves on each side panel, and using the pilot holes previously drilled in each side panel, screw and glue the end and side panels together.

8 Make and glue two corner blocks 294mm (11½in) long, 12mm (½in) sq in position as shown (Fig 1).

Fig 3

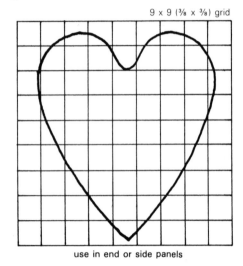

9 x 9 (⅜ x ⅜) grid

use in end or side panels

Cutting list

Base	1 off	584×306×3mm (23×12×⅛in)	Plywood
End panel	2 off	432×359×12mm (17×14⅛×½in)	Plywood
Side panel	2 off	584×232×12mm (23×9⅛×½in)	Plywood
Corner blocks	2 off	294×12×12mm (11½×½×½in)	Wood

Ancillaries

Screws	4 off	35mm (1¼in) long×No 8	Bright zinc
Cup washers	4 off	suitable for No 8 screws	Bright zinc

TOY BOX

With children in the house, there are bound to be lots of toys lying around that never seem to stay tidy for more than five minutes. Although cardboard boxes can be very useful for storing toys they inevitably collapse, leaving their contents strewn all over the floor.

This toy box is a good strong box which is easy for children to reach into for their favourite toy, and is also light enough to be moved around on its castors from one play area to another. When painted in your child's favourite colours, it will make an attractive and very practical accessory to any nursery or playroom.

The usefulness of this toy box doesn't end when the children have finished with it. Its life span can be increased with another quick coat of paint and possibly a lid, which will immediately turn it into a blanket box for extra storage needs.

To add a touch of individualism and originality to your toy box, card stencils of various patterns suitable for children are available. Suppliers of these stencils usually advertise in home improvement magazines.

1 Cut to size the base panel (Fig 1), the two end panels (Fig 2) and the two side panels (Fig 3).

2 Four battens (see Cutting List) are now cut to length and screwed and glued through countersunk holes to the underside of the base (Fig 1).

3 Using a flat bit, drill two 12mm (½in) dia holes in each end panel (Fig 2). For method, see Hand Tools (page 10).

4 Cut to length, and screw and glue two beechwood corner blocks (see cutting list) to each end panel.

Because beech is a hardwood, it is necessary to drill pilot holes in the relevant positions (see Fig 2 and Fig 3) in each corner block to help with assembly and avoid splitting when screwed to the side and end panels.

5 Drill and countersink eight 4mm (³⁄₁₆in) dia holes in each side panel.

6 To assemble toy box place the base panel on a flat surface and stand one end panel upright in position alongside it. Then screw and glue the two panels together. Repeat this procedure with the remaining three panels.

7 All that remains to be done now is to screw on the castors and fit the handles. The castors are screwed underneath at each corner, and the rope handles are inserted and tied through the 12mm (½in) holes on each end panel.

Cutting list

Base	1 off	890×432×12mm (35×17×½in)	Plywood
Battens	2 off	890×35×18mm (35×1⅜×¾in)	Wood
Battens	2 off	362×35×18mm (14¼×1⅜×¾in)	Wood
End panels	2 off	356×432×12mm (14×17×½in)	Plywood
Corner blocks	4 off	326×18×18mm (12¾×¾×¾in)	Beechwood
Side panels	2 off	356×914×12mm (14×36×½in)	Plywood

Ancillaries

Castors	4 off	32mm (1¼in) dia plate type
Rope handles		12mm (½in) dia length as desired

Fig 1 Assembled base

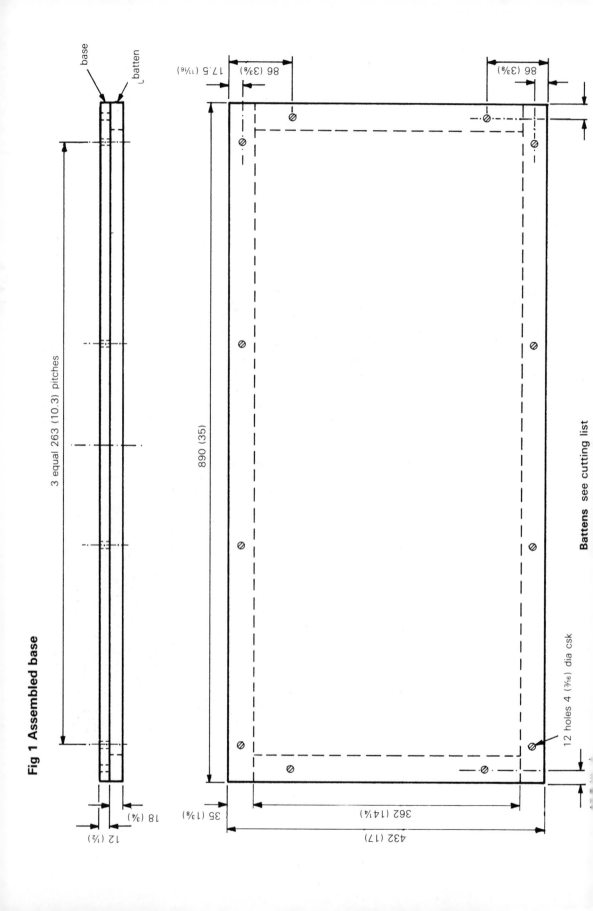

base

batten

3 equal 263 (10.3) pitches

12 (½)

18 (¾)

35 (1⅜)

17.5 (11⁄16)

86 (3⅜)

86 (3⅜)

890 (35)

362 (14¼)

432 (17)

12 holes 4 (³⁄₁₆) dia csk

Battens see cutting list

Fig 2 End panel
make two

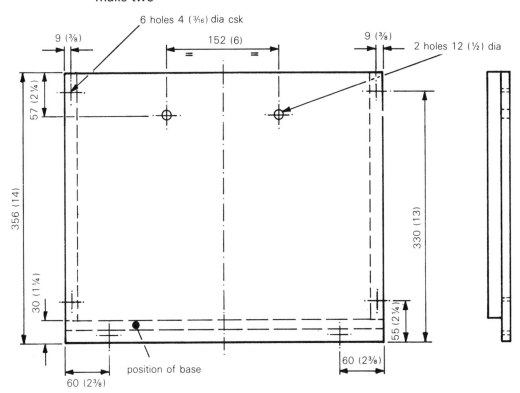

6 holes 4 (³/₁₆) dia csk

9 (³/₈)

152 (6)

9 (³/₈)

2 holes 12 (½) dia

57 (2¼)

356 (14)

30 (1¼)

330 (13)

55 (2¼)

60 (2³/₈)

position of base

60 (2³/₈)

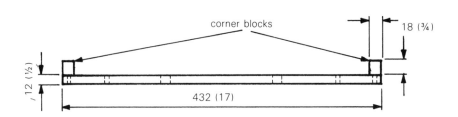

corner blocks

18 (¾)

12 (½)

432 (17)

Corner blocks see cutting list

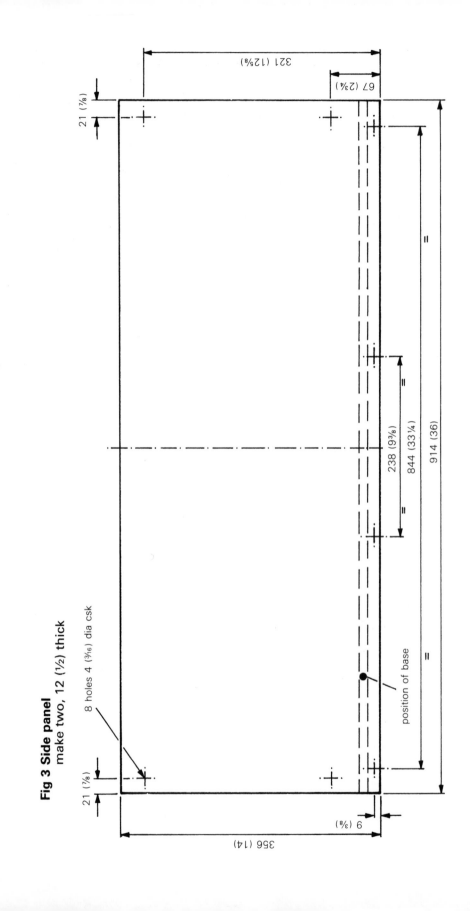

Fig 3 Side panel
make two, 12 (½) thick

8 holes 4 (³⁄₁₆) dia csk

position of base

321 (12⅝)

67 (2¾)

21 (⅞)

238 (9⅜)

844 (33¼)

914 (36)

21 (⅞)

356 (14)

9 (³⁄₈)

COTTAGE NIGHT LIGHT/MONEY BOX

For some children, a night light is an important part of going to bed. Leaving an ordinary light on can be distracting for the child, and expensive for the parents. This night light has been designed with both these factors in mind. A low wattage light bulb (15 watts) gives the child enough light to see the surrounding room without keeping him or her awake and saves electricity at the same time.

It is essential that a project such as this should be made with safety in mind. Children's curiosity is naturally aroused by things they do not understand, and they must be protected from danger, especially where electricity is concerned. For this reason, the roof must be securely screwed in place with four screws (see Fig 4) and the perspex used for the windows must be at least 1.5mm (1/16in) thick. A good contact adhesive should be used when fixing the windows to the walls.

When your children no longer require a night light, this project can then be converted into a money box. To do this, simply remove all of the electrical equipment from inside and cut a narrow slot in one of the roof panels and, hey presto, you have a cottage money box. If your children are too old for a night light, why not make it as a money box to begin with?

1 As will be seen from the drawings, the base (Fig 1), the walls (Figs 2 and 3) and the roof sections (Fig 4) each have tags. When cutting out these parts try to be as accurate as possible.

2 Mark and cut out the base (Fig 1), the front and back walls (Fig 2) and the two end walls (Fig 3). The cable entry hole shown on Fig 3 is only to be drilled on one end wall. If you are not sure how to make the window openings, refer to Methods and Materials (page 8).

Fig 1 Base
6 (¼) thick

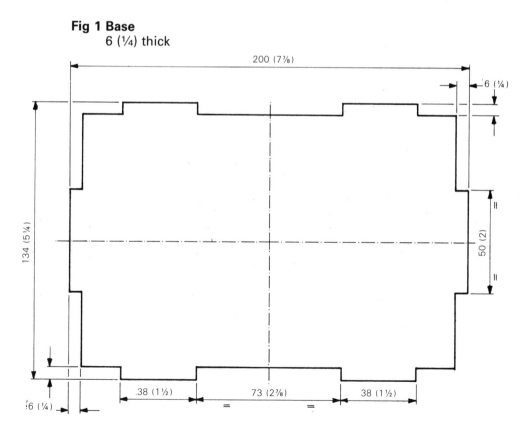

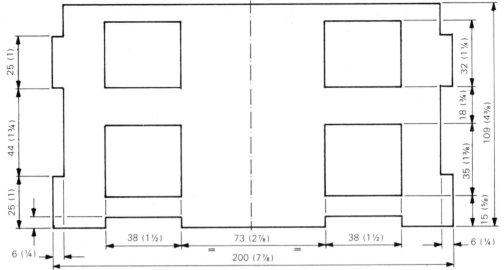

Fig 2 Front/back wall
make one each, 6 (¼) thick

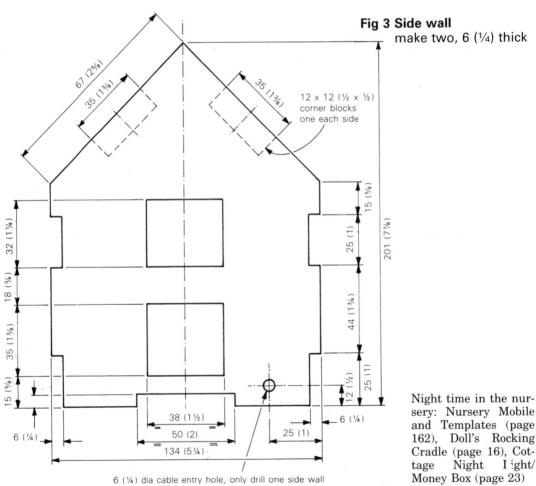

Fig 3 Side wall
make two, 6 (¼) thick

12 x 12 (½ x ½)
corner blocks
one each side

6 (¼) dia cable entry hole, only drill one side wall

Night time in the nursery: Nursery Mobile and Templates (page 162), Doll's Rocking Cradle (page 16), Cottage Night Light/ Money Box (page 23)

Fig 4 Roof sections
make one of each, 6 (¼) thick

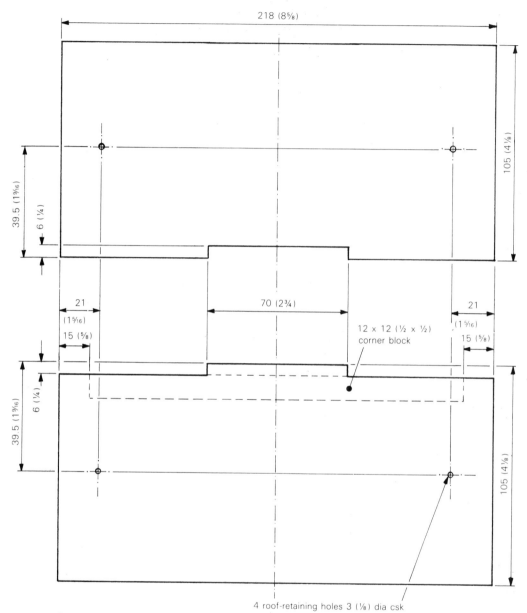

218 (8⅝)

105 (4⅛)

39.5 (1⁹⁄₁₆)

6 (¼)

21

(1⁵⁄₁₆)

15 (⅝)

70 (2¾)

12 x 12 (½ x ½)
corner block

21

(1⁵⁄₁₆)

15 (⅝)

39.5 (1⁹⁄₁₆)

6 (¼)

105 (4⅛)

4 roof-retaining holes 3 (⅛) dia csk

Corner block 188 x 12 x 12 (7⅜ x ½ x ½) wood

previous page Rescue Centre (page 41)

Doll's Buggy (page 55), Sit 'n Ride Fire Engine
(page 146)

Fig 5 Lamp holder fixing block

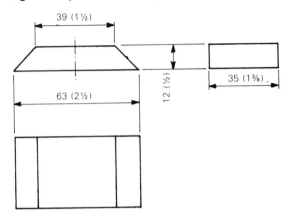

Fig 6 Chimney stack

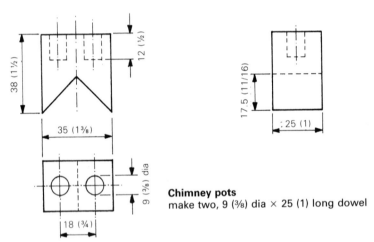

Chimney pots
make two, 9 (⅜) dia × 25 (1) long dowel

3 Before any glue is applied, dry assemble the parts you have already cut out. If a joint is stiff, use a file to ease it.

4 Glue the walls and base together. Allow glue to harden before glueing two corner blocks to each end wall (Fig 3).

5 Cut out and assemble the two roof sections (Fig 4), and glue the lamp holder fixing block (Fig 5) in such a position that the combined length of your lamp holder and light bulb does not obstruct the side walls when the cottage is assembled (see also Fig 8).

6 Drill 9mm (⅜in) dia holes in the chimney stack (Fig 6) before cutting the bottom to shape.

7 Cut the two chimney pot dowels to length, and glue them in position.

8 When making the replica beams (Fig 8), paint them before glueing them in position.

9 Cut the window panels to size. Place them in their respective positions inside the assembled cottage and mark the window positions onto them. Using an indelible marker pen, draw the replica leaded windows onto the window panels. Use contact adhesive to fix the panels in place inside the cottage.

10 Using thin gauge steel sheet, make the lamp holder bracket (Fig 7). The lamp holder fixing holes and cable entry holes

Fig 7 Lamp holder bracket
(steel)

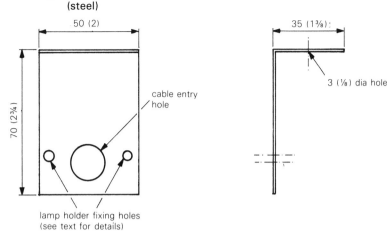

50 (2)

70 (2¾)

35 (1⅜)

cable entry hole

3 (⅛) dia hole

lamp holder fixing holes
(see text for details)

Fig 8 Assembled roof

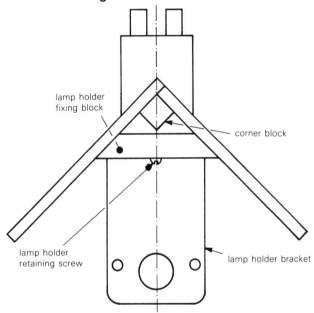

lamp holder
fixing block

corner block

lamp holder
retaining screw

lamp holder bracket

are not dimensioned as these will depend entirely on the type of lamp holder you are using.

11 When connecting the electric cable, ensure all connections are tight. Leave enough cable inside the cottage so that the roof can be removed easily. It is important to restrain the cable inside the cottage so that it does not pull out; this is done by simply tying a knot in the cable.

The earth wire (green and yellow) must be connected to the metal lamp holder bracket. This is done by placing two flat washers onto the lamp holder retaining screw and making the connection between the washers.

12 Make sure the roof is screwed in position before placing the night light in your child's bedroom.

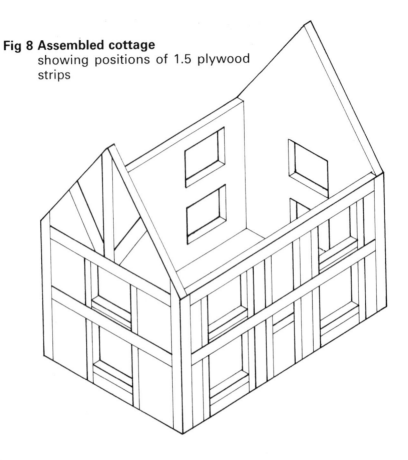

Fig 8 Assembled cottage
showing positions of 1.5 plywood strips

Cutting list

Base	1 off	200×134×6mm (7⅞×5¼×¼in)	Plywood
Front/Back walls	1 off each	200×109×6mm (7⅞×4⅜×¼in)	Plywood
End walls	2 off	134×201×6mm (5¼×7⅞×¼in)	Plywood
Corner blocks	4 off	35×12×12mm (1⅜×½×½in)	Wood
Roof	2 off	105×218×6mm (8⅝×4⅛×¼in)	Plywood
Roof corner block	1 off	188×12×12mm (7⅜×½×½in)	Plywood
Lamp holder-fixing block	1 off	63×35×12mm (2½×1⅜×½in)	Wood
Chimney stack	1 off	35×38×25mm (1⅜×1½×1in)	Wood
Chimney pots	2 off	9mm (⅜in) dia×25mm (1in) long dowel	
Replica beams	various lengths of both 6mm (¼in) wide and 9mm (⅜in) wide× 1mm (1/32in) thick (see Fig 8)		

Ancillaries

Electric cable		0.5mm sq 3 core	length as required
Electric plug top		type as required	
Light bulb holder		type as required	
Lamp holder bracket		50×70×0.5mm (2×2¾×1/32in)	Steel
Light bulb		15 watts maximum	
Roof retaining screws	4 off	No 4×12mm (½in)	Bright zinc
	4 off	cup washers	Bright zinc
Window panels	2 off	188×102×1.5mm (7⅜×4×1/16in)	Perspex
	2 off	114×94×1.5mm (4½×3¾×1/16in)	Perspex

STALWART AMPHIBIOUS TRUCK

The Stalwart is a general service, 5-ton, six-wheeled drive, high mobility load carrier, and is three vehicles in one. It is a conventional road vehicle, a cross-country vehicle and also an amphibious vehicle. When used in its amphibious role, independent water propulsion is supplied by two Dowty marine jet units. The Stalwart was first introduced into the British Army in 1966.

As a high mobility load carrier the Stalwart has many varied uses, such as recovery vehicle, missile carrier, beach loading logistical vehicle, troop carrier and many more. These variations can, if desired, be adapted to your model by using photographs of other vehicles. Your local library is a good source of information.

As with the original Stalwart, this model, in spite of its finished weight, is also an amphibian. It is essential therefore to use waterproof materials throughout its construction. Polystyrene blocks

Fig 1 Assembled views

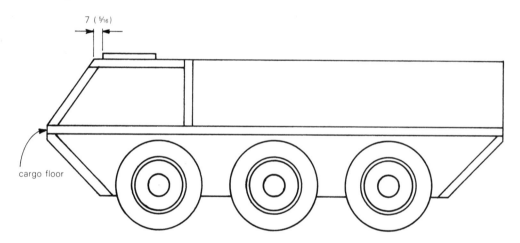

7 (⁵⁄₁₆)

cargo floor

Fig 2 Hatches

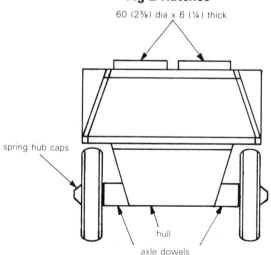

60 (2⅜) dia x 6 (¼) thick

spring hub caps

hull

axle dowels

Fig 3 Assembled views

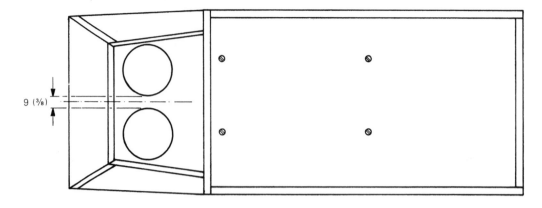

Fig 4 Hull formers
make two, 9 (⅜) thick

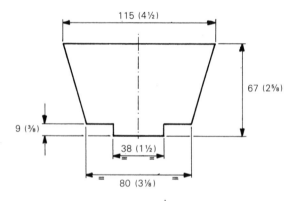

cut to shape and placed inside the hull during construction will displace any water that may enter through the axle holes.

Most parts for the Stalwart model have to be cut at an angle (see drawings), and an electrical jigsaw which has an adjustable sole plate to cut angles will be very useful to you, but it is not essential. If you are using a jigsaw, make test cuts using 9mm (⅜in) thick scrap wood before cutting the part required.

Some parts are shown over size; this is to allow for edges to be shaped.

1 Using the methods described above, mark and cut out the hull base (Fig 5). Before cutting out the hull base, mark the positions of the axle centres on its underside (see Fig 6). This will ensure accurate alignment when drilling the axle holes later. Refer to Methods and Materials (page 8) if you are unsure how to make the two hull former location slots shown on Fig 5.

2 Mark and cut out the hull formers (Fig 4) and glue them in position.

3 Place a block of polystyrene on the base, against a hull former. Draw around the former onto the polystyrene. Cut the polystyrene to shape and cut the middle section to length 165mm (6½in). Do not cut the end sections to length at this time.

4 Mark and cut out the hull sides (Fig 6). Pin and glue them in position.

5 Place the remaining shaped polystyrene

Fig 5 Hull base

9 (⅜)

80 (3⅛)

73°

45°

386 (15¼)

38 (1½)

9 (⅜)

165 (6½)

9 (⅜)

hull former location slots

Fig 6 Hull sides
make two, 9 (⅜) thick

73°

12 (½)

73 (2⅞)

chamfer to suit hull end panel
when assembled

506 (19¾)

259 (10¼)

372 (14⅝)

chamfer to suit
hull end panels when
assembled

three 6 (¼) dia holes

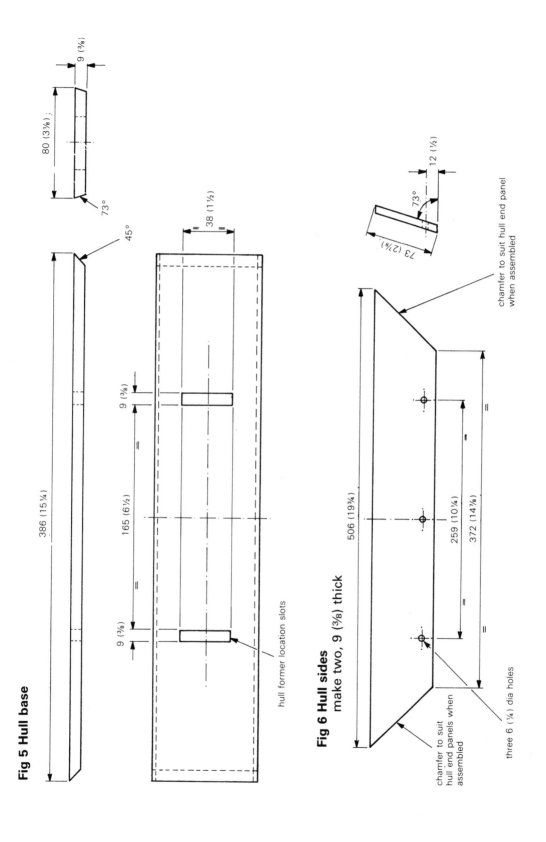

Fig 7 Hull end panels
make two

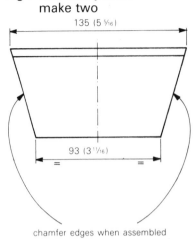

135 (5 ⁵/₁₆)

93 (3 ¹¹/₁₆)

chamfer edges when assembled

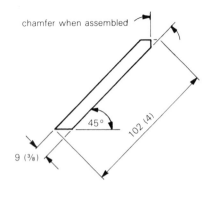

chamfer when assembled

45°

102 (4)

9 (³/₈)

Fig 8 Cab/cargo floor

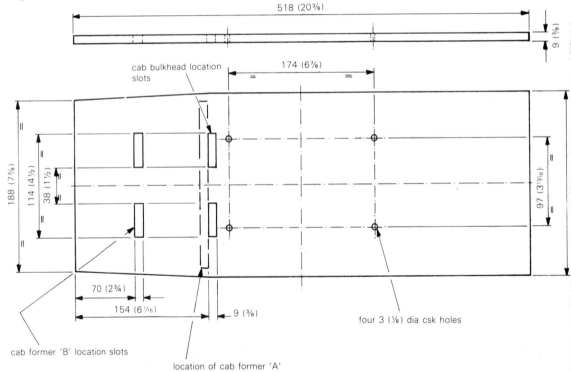

518 (20³/₈)

9 (³/₈)

cab bulkhead location slots

174 (6⁷/₈)

188 (7³/₈)

114 (4½)

38 (1½)

97 (3¹³/₁₆)

70 (2¾)

154 (6¹/₁₆)

9 (³/₈)

four 3 (¹/₈) dia csk holes

cab former 'B' location slots

location of cab former 'A'

Fig 9 Cab bulkhead
9 (3/8) thick

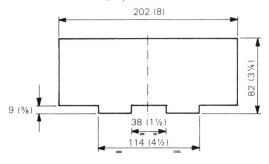

Fig 10 Cab former 'A'
9 (3/8) thick

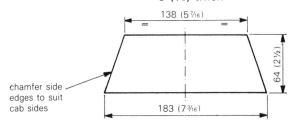

Fig 11 Cab former 'B'

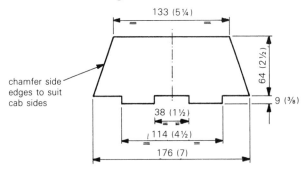

Fig 12 Cab side
make one of each hand

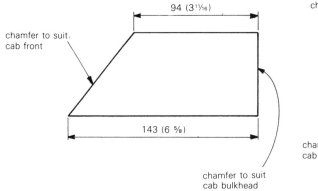
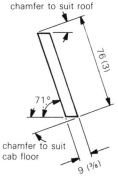

Fig 13 Cab front

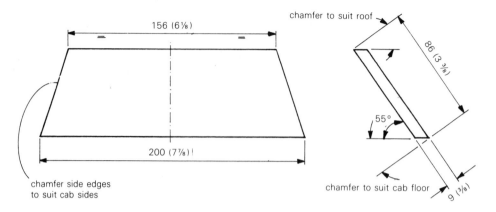

156 (6⅛)

200 (7⅞)!

chamfer side edges
to suit cab sides

chamfer to suit roof

86 (3⅜)

55°

chamfer to suit cab floor

9 (⅜)

Fig 14 Cab roof

chamfer to suit
cab front

9 (⅜)

106 (4³⁄₁₆)

158 (6¼)

150 (5⅞)

chamber to
suit cab sides

blocks inside the partly assembled hull. Using the hull sides as a guide, now cut the polystyrene to length and shape.

6 Mark and cut out the hull end panels (Fig 7). Pin and glue them in position. These can be cut over size and chamfered to shape when in position.

7 Glue and screw the cab/cargo floor (Fig 8) in position on top of the assembled hull.

Mark and use centre lines to locate the two parts correctly.

8 Cut out, and glue in position, the cab bulkhead (Fig 9).

9 Cab formers 'A' and 'B' (Figs 10 and 11) should be placed in position only (see Fig 8) at this time, until they have been dry assembled with the cab sides and checked for accuracy.

10 Cut, shape, and glue into position the cab front (Fig 13), followed by the cab roof (Fig 14). The edges of these parts should be shaped to the existing cab when in position.
11 Stand the so far assembled model on its side. Mark and drill three axle holes vertically on each side of the hull. Cut the axles to length and insert them into the hull.

12 Make the axle dowels (Fig 17), slide them onto the axles and glue in place.
13 Mark, cut out and glue into position the cargo sides (Figs 15 and 16), and the cab hatches (Fig 2).
14 When fitting the wheels, place a flat washer between each wheel and axle block.
15 Refer to Figs 18 and 18a when marking out cab window positions.

Cutting list

Hull formers (Fig 4)	2 off	115×67×9mm (4½×2⅝×⅜in)	Plywood
Hull base (Fig 5)	1 off	386×80×9mm (15¼×3⅛×⅜in)	Plywood
Hull sides (Fig 6)	2 off	506×73×9mm (19¾×2⅞×⅜in)	Plywood
Hull end panels (Fig 7)	2 off	135×102×9mm (5⁵⁄₁₆×4×⅜in)	Plywood
Cab/cargo floor (Fig 8)	1 off	518×202×9mm (20⅜×8×⅜in)	Plywood
Cab bulkhead (Fig 9)	1 off	202×82×9mm (8×3¼×⅜in)	Plywood
Cab former 'A' (Fig 10)	1 off	183×64×9mm (7³⁄₁₆×2½×⅜in)	Plywood
Cab former 'B' (Fig 11)	1 off	176×73×9mm (7×2⅞×⅜in)	Plywood
Cab sides (Fig 12)	2 off	143×76×9mm (6⅝×3×⅜in)	Plywood
Cab front (Fig 13)	1 off	200×86×9mm (7⅞×3⅜×⅜in)	Plywood
Cab roof (Fig 14)	1 off	158×106×9mm (6¼×4³⁄₁₆×⅜in)	Plywood
Axle dowels (Fig 17)	6 off	28mm (1⅛in) long×25mm (1in) diameter dowel	
Cargo sides (Fig 15)	2 off	355×73×9mm (13¹⁵⁄₁₆×2⅞×⅜in)	Plywood
(Fig 16)	2 off	184×73×9mm (7¼×2⅞×⅜in)	Plywood

Ancillaries

Polystyrene		506×115×67mm (19¾×4½×2⅝)	
Axles	3 off	226mm (8⅜in) long×6mm (¼in) dia steel rod	
Wheels	6 off	102mm (4in) dia (axle dia 6mm (¼in))	
Spring hub caps	6 off	to suit 6mm (¼in) dia axle	
Flat washers	6 off	inside dia 6mm (¼in)	
Bright zinc panel pins		18mm (¾in) long	

Fig 15 Cargo sides
make two of each, 9 (⅜) thick

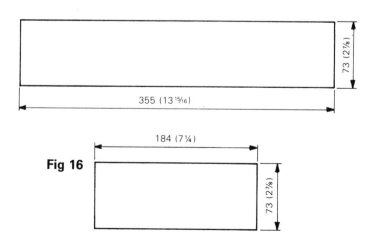

73 (2⅞)

355 (13¹⁵⁄₁₆)

184 (7¼)

Fig 16

73 (2⅞)

Fig 17 Axle dowels
make 6

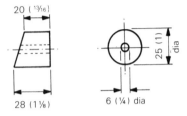

20 (¹³⁄₁₆)

28 (1⅛)

25 (1) dia

6 (¼) dia

Fig 18 Assembled cab
window positions

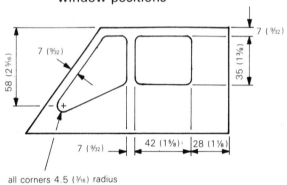

7 (⁹⁄₃₂)

7 (⁹⁄₃₂)

58 (2⁵⁄₁₆)

35 (1⅜)

7 (⁹⁄₃₂)

42 (1⅝) 28 (1⅛)

all corners 4.5 (³⁄₁₆) radius

Fig 18a

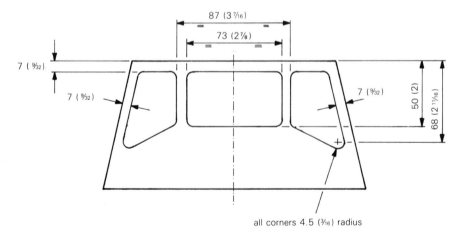

87 (3⁷⁄₁₆)

73 (2⅞)

7 (⁹⁄₃₂)

7 (⁹⁄₃₂)

7 (⁹⁄₃₂)

50 (2)

68 (2¹¹⁄₁₆)

all corners 4.5 (³⁄₁₆) radius

RESCUE CENTRE

Emergency vehicles have always held a fascination for children, possibly because of the bright colours in which they are painted, or maybe because of the noises they make. For whatever reason emergency vehicles stimulate a child's imagination, and are certainly very individual, requiring their own garaging facilities.

This project brings together the real world of busy fire, police and ambulance stations into the living room, and the child's vivid imagination closer to reality. A helicopter landing pad with hangar and control tower facilities has been provided on top of the ambulance station for aerial rescues. Firemen can practise their rescue techniques on top of the fire station using the training tower.

When making this project, you can decide how many of the three units you would like to make, and how many doors you would like to make operable if you do

not have time to make them all. Maybe you would like to add more helipads to the roofs; this can also be done.

Throughout the drawings reference is made to 'cladding'; this is simulated by using reed moulding. Reed moulding was only available in four reed, 22mm (⅞in) wide, so to make six reed cladding, 33mm (1⁵⁄₁₆in) wide, cut two lengths of four reed to the required size, and split one length in half with a sharp trimming knife.

1 Mark and cut out the three bases (Figs 1 and 2) and mark the positions of the front and back walls on each base. Chamfer the leading edges up to the marks so that a toy car can enter and leave the base easily. To chamfer, wrap a piece of rough abrasive paper (about 80 grit) around a flat file or block of wood. When completed, smooth the chamfered area with fine glass paper.

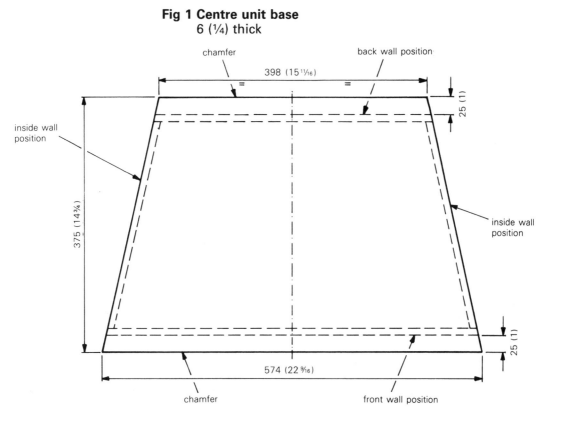

Fig 1 Centre unit base
6 (¼) thick

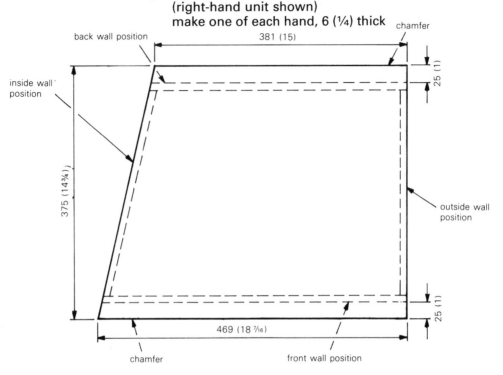

Fig 2 Side units base
(right-hand unit shown)
make one of each hand, 6 (¼) thick

back wall position

inside wall position

381 (15)

chamfer

25 (1)

375 (14¾)

outside wall position

469 (18 ⁷⁄₁₆)

25 (1)

chamfer

front wall position

2 Mark and cut out the centre unit front and back walls (Figs 3 and 4). Do not chamfer the edges of these walls until all the centre unit walls have been screwed and glued to the base. Make door openings as described in Methods and Materials (page 8).

3 Cut to size the roof support blocks and door stops. Glue them in their respective positions on the inside face of each wall.

4 Using the previously marked wall positions as a guide, drill and countersink 4mm (³⁄₁₆in) dia wall securing holes in the centre unit base. Screw and glue the front and back walls in position.

5 Cut out the roof, and temporarily screw it into position across the assembled front and back walls. This procedure will retain the shape of the building while the inside walls are being fitted.

6 Mark and cut out the inside walls (Fig 5). Chamfer the edges of these walls until they fit between the front and back walls (see Fig 1), then screw and glue them in position. When the glue has hardened, chamfer the front and back walls to suit.

7 Make up door guide assemblies and guide stops (Fig 6). Guide stops should only be glued to the door guides when painting has been completed and doors inserted into door guides. For smooth operation of the doors, use a hardwood such as beech when making the door guide assemblies.

8 Mark the positions of the door guides on the roof (Fig 8), and screw and glue them in position as shown in Fig 7.

9 Screw and glue the roof in position on top of the roof support blocks.

10 Glue the guide spacers (Fig 6) in position against the front and back walls. These will stop the door runners 4mm (³⁄₁₆in) short of the walls and enable the doors to close without catching the top of the door frame.

11 Make up the door runner assemblies (Fig 9), rounding the ends of the steel rods.

12 Mark and cut out the centre unit front and back doors (Figs 11 and 12). Glue two door runner assemblies in position on each door. Before painting the doors,

Fig 3 Centre unit, front wall
9 (⅜) thick

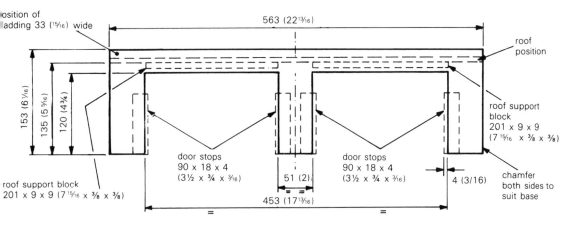

position of cladding 33 (¹⁵⁄₁₆) wide

563 (22¹³⁄₁₆)

roof position

153 (6¹⁄₁₆)
135 (5⁵⁄₁₆)
120 (4¾)

roof support block
201 x 9 x 9
(7 ¹⁵⁄₁₆ x ⅜ x ⅜)

door stops
90 x 18 x 4
(3½ x ¾ x ³⁄₁₆)

door stops
90 x 18 x 4
(3½ x ¾ x ³⁄₁₆)

51 (2)

4 (3/16)

chamfer
both sides to
suit base

roof support block
201 x 9 x 9 (7 ¹⁵⁄₁₆ x ⅜ x ⅜)

453 (17¹³⁄₁₆)

Fig 4 Centre unit, back wall
9 (⅜) thick

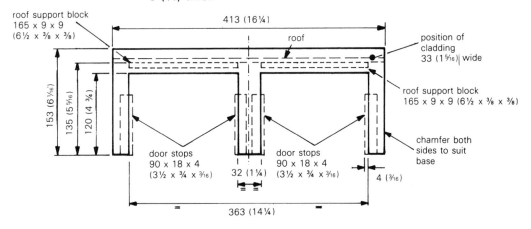

roof support block
165 x 9 x 9
(6½ x ⅜ x ⅜)

413 (16¼)

roof

position of
cladding
33 (1⁵⁄₁₆) wide

153 (6¹⁄₁₆)
135 (5⁵⁄₁₆)
120 (4 ¾)

roof support block
165 x 9 x 9 (6½ x ⅜ x ⅜)

door stops
90 x 18 x 4
(3½ x ¾ x ³⁄₁₆)

32 (1¼)

door stops
90 x 18 x 4
(3½ x ¾ x ³⁄₁₆)

4 (³⁄₁₆)

chamfer both
sides to suit
base

363 (14¼)

Fig 5 Inside walls
9 (⅜) thick
make two for centre unit
make one for each side unit

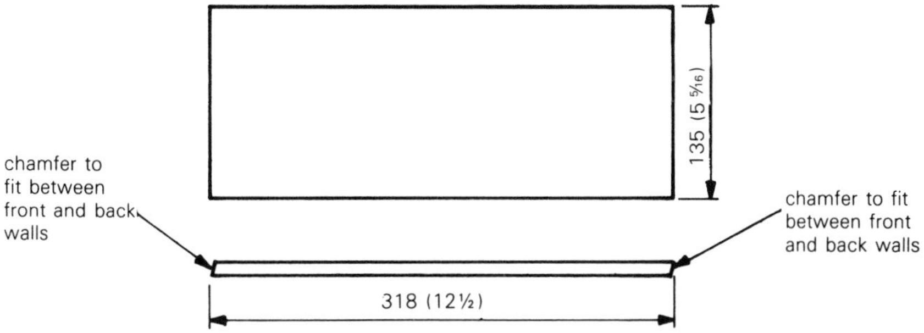

135 (5⁵⁄₁₆)

chamfer to
fit between
front and back
walls

chamfer to fit
between front
and back walls

318 (12½)

43

Fig 6 Door guide stop assemblies
make twelve of each hand (right-hand guide shown)

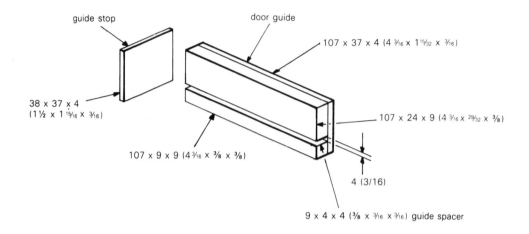

guide stop

door guide

107 x 37 x 4 (4 ³⁄₁₆ x 1¹⁵⁄₃₂ x ³⁄₁₆)

38 x 37 x 4
(1½ x 1¹⁵⁄₁₆ x ³⁄₁₆)

107 x 24 x 9 (4 ³⁄₁₆ x ²⁹⁄₃₂ x ³⁄₈)

107 x 9 x 9 (4 ³⁄₁₆ x ³⁄₈ x ³⁄₈)

4 (3/16)

9 x 4 x 4 (³⁄₈ x ³⁄₁₆ x ³⁄₁₆) guide spacer

Fig 7 Front view of assembled door guide with door in open position
(part of wall has been removed)

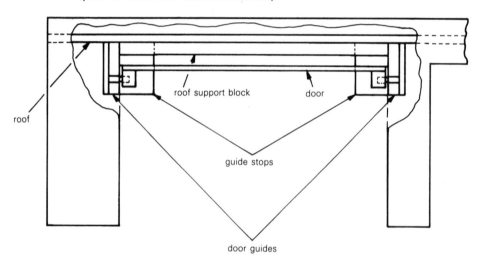

roof support block

door

roof

guide stops

door guides

Fig 8 Centre unit, roof
6 (¼) thick, showing door guide positions

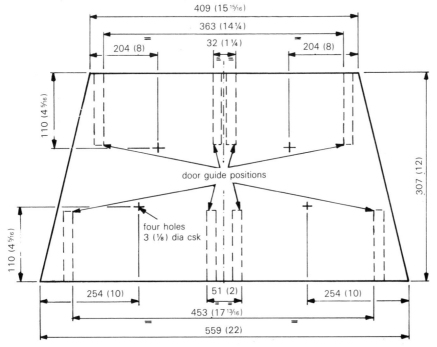

door guide positions

four holes
3 (⅛) dia csk

Fig 9 Door runner assembly
make twenty-four

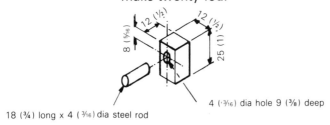

18 (¾) long x 4 (³⁄₁₆) dia steel rod

4 (·³⁄₁₆) dia hole 9 (⅜) deep

Fig 10 Assembled door rest
make twelve

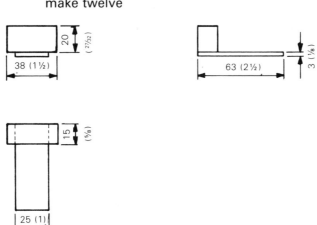

Fig 11 Centre unit, front doors
showing door runners in position
make two, 4 (³⁄₁₆) thick

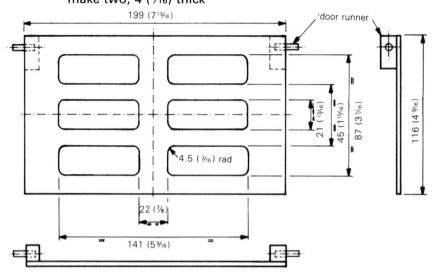

door runner

199 (7¹³⁄₁₆)

21 (¹³⁄₁₆)
45 (1¹⁵⁄₁₆)
87 (3⁷⁄₁₆)

116 (4⁹⁄₁₆)

4.5 (³⁄₁₆) rad

22 (⅞)

141 (5⁹⁄₁₆)

Fig 12 Centre unit, back doors
door runner positions as Fig 10
make two, 4 (³⁄₁₆) thick

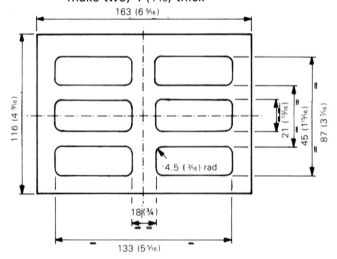

163 (6⁵⁄₁₆)

116 (4⁹⁄₁₆)

21 (¹³⁄₁₆)
45 (1¹⁵⁄₁₆)
87 (3⁷⁄₁₆)

4.5 (³⁄₁₆) rad

18 (¾)

133 (5⁵⁄₁₆)

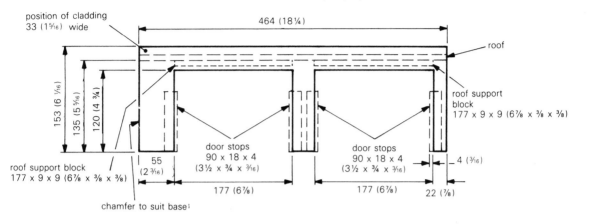

Fig 13 Side unit, front walls
(right-hand unit shown)
make one of each hand, 9 (⅜) thick

position of cladding
33 (1⁵⁄₁₆) wide

464 (18¼)

roof

153 (6¹⁄₁₆)

135 (5⁵⁄₁₆)

120 (4¾)

roof support
block
177 x 9 x 9 (6⅞ x ⅜ x ⅜)

roof support block
177 x 9 x 9 (6⅞ x ⅜ x ⅜)

55
(2³⁄₁₆)

door stops
90 x 18 x 4
(3½ x ¾ x ³⁄₁₆)

door stops
90 x 18 x 4
(3½ x ¾ x ³⁄₁₆)

4 (³⁄₁₆)

177 (6⅞)

177 (6⅞)

22 (⅞)

chamfer to suit base

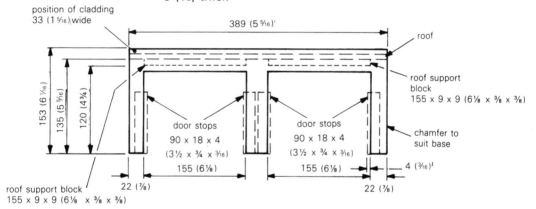

Fig 14 Right-hand side unit, back wall
9 (⅜) thick

position of cladding
33 (1⁵⁄₁₆) wide

389 (5⁵⁄₁₆)

roof

153 (6¹⁄₁₆)

135 (5⁵⁄₁₆)

120 (4¾)

roof support
block
155 x 9 x 9 (6⅛ x ⅜ x ⅜)

door stops
90 x 18 x 4
(3½ x ¾ x ³⁄₁₆)

door stops
90 x 18 x 4
(3½ x ¾ x ³⁄₁₆)

chamfer to
suit base

155 (6⅛)

155 (6⅛)

4 (³⁄₁₆)

roof support block
155 x 9 x 9 (6⅛ x ⅜ x ⅜)

22 (⅞)

22 (⅞)

Inside wall (see Fig 5)

check them for smooth operation in their respective guides. A total of twelve doors have to be made altogether, and it is a good idea to number each door as it is made and fitted.

13 Either side unit can now be made, but following the order of the plans, make the right-hand unit (see photo page 26) next. Assemble side units in the same way as centre unit.

14 When making up the side unit outside walls (Figs 15 and 22), glue two door guide assemblies (Fig 6) in position on each wall.

15 Mark and cut out the training tower side wall (Fig 16) and screw and glue it in position (see Fig 19).

16 Screw and glue door guides to roof (Fig 19). Then screw and glue the roof in place.

17 Cut to size the four training tower cross beams (Fig 17) and glue them in position.

18 Mark and cut out the two training tower floors (Fig 18) and glue them in position underneath the cross beams. When fixing the cladding to the training tower mitre the joints.

19 Cut out the remaining doors (Figs 20 and 21). Assemble, and test them for ease of operation.

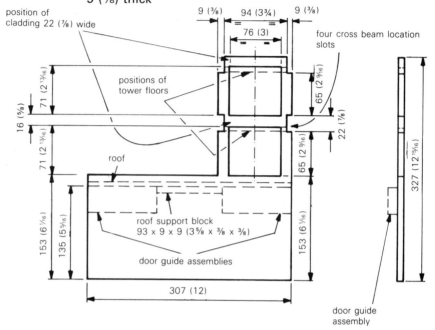

Fig 15 Right-hand unit, outside wall with training tower
9 (³⁄₈) thick

position of
cladding 22 (⁷⁄₈) wide

9 (³⁄₈)   94 (3¾)   9 (³⁄₈)

76 (3)

four cross beam location
slots

positions of
tower floors

71 (2¹³⁄₁₆)

16 (⁵⁄₈)

65 (2⁹⁄₁₆)

71 (2¹³⁄₁₆)

22 (⁷⁄₈)

roof

65 (2⁹⁄₁₆)

153 (6¹⁄₁₆)

135 (5⁹⁄₁₆)

roof support block
93 x 9 x 9 (3⁵⁄₈ x ³⁄₈ x ³⁄₈)

door guide assemblies

153 (6¹⁄₁₆)

327 (12¹⁵⁄₁₆)

307 (12)

door guide
assembly

Fig 16 Training tower, side wall
9 (³⁄₈) thick

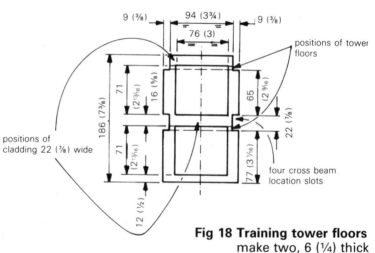

9 (³⁄₈)   94 (3¾)   9 (³⁄₈)

76 (3)

positions of tower
floors

positions of
cladding 22 (⁷⁄₈) wide

186 (7³⁄₈)

71
(2¹³⁄₁₆)

16 (⁵⁄₈)

65
(2⁹⁄₁₆)

22 (⁷⁄₈)

71
(2¹³⁄₁₆)

77 (3¹⁄₁₆)

four cross beam
location slots

12 (½)

Fig 18 Training tower floors
make two, 6 (¼) thick

Fig 17 Training tower, cross beams
make four, 9 (³⁄₈) thick

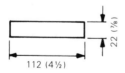

22 (⁷⁄₈)

112 (4½)

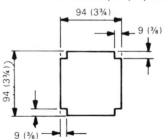

94 (3¾)

9 (³⁄₈)

94 (3¾)

9 (³⁄₈)

Fig 19 Right-hand side unit, roof
6 (¾) thick

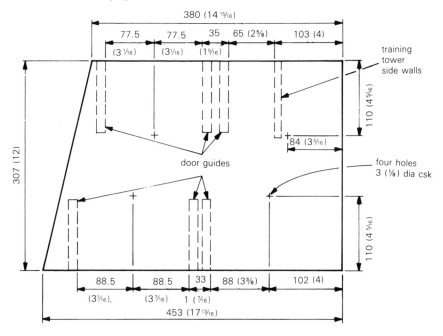

Fig 20 Side unit, back doors
door runners as Fig 10
make four, 4 (³⁄₁₆) thick

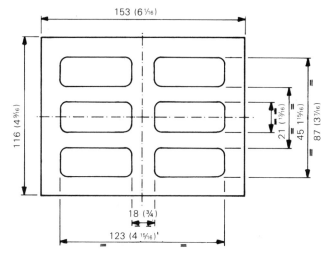

Fig 21 Side unit, front doors
make four, 6 (¼) thick

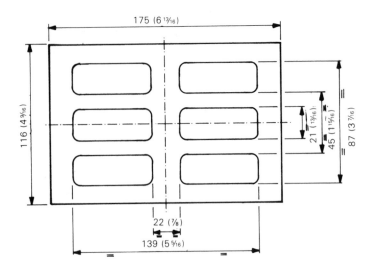

Fig 22 Left-hand unit, outside wall
9 (⅜) thick

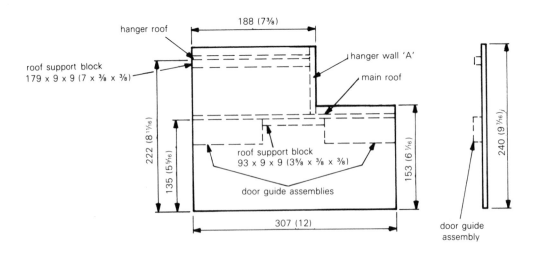

20 Cut out and assemble left-hand unit. Use vertical and horizontal corner blocks inside the hangar. This will add strength to hangar walls 'A' and 'B'.

21 Make up and glue in position the cladding for all units.

22 Mark and cut out the control tower parts (Figs 29–34). Glue the back, and side walls in position on the hangar roof as shown in Fig 28. Paint the inside of the control tower before glueing the roof and perspex window panels in position.

23 Cut to size and assemble the twelve door rests (Fig 10). These rests are to keep the doors in an open position, and therefore they should be tested against each open door before they are screwed and glued in position.

Fig 23 Left-hand side unit, back wall
9 (³⁄₈) thick

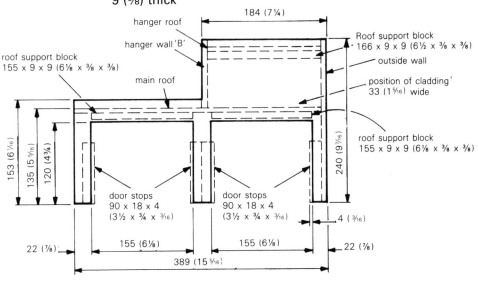

hanger roof

hanger wall 'B'

roof support block
155 x 9 x 9 (6⅛ x ³⁄₈ x ³⁄₈)

main roof

Roof support block
166 x 9 x 9 (6½ x ³⁄₈ x ³⁄₈)

outside wall

position of cladding
33 (1⁵⁄₁₆) wide

roof support block
155 x 9 x 9 (6⅛ x ³⁄₈ x ³⁄₈)

184 (7¼)

153 (6¹⁄₁₆)

135 (5⁵⁄₁₆)

120 (4¾)

240 (9⁷⁄₁₆)

door stops
90 x 18 x 4
(3½ x ¾ x ³⁄₁₆)

door stops
90 x 18 x 4
(3½ x ¾ x ³⁄₁₆)

4 (³⁄₁₆)

22 (⅞)

155 (6⅛)

155 (6⅛)

22 (⅞)

389 (15⁵⁄₁₆)

Fig 24 Left-hand unit, main roof
showing door guide positions
6 (¾) thick

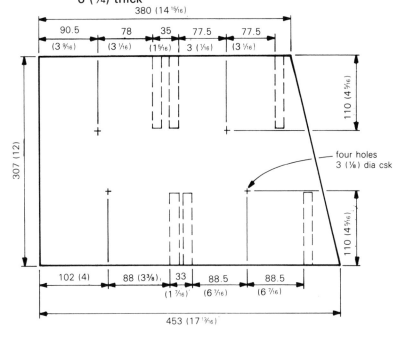

380 (14¹⁵⁄₁₆)

90.5
(3⁹⁄₁₆)

78
(3¹⁄₁₆)

35
(1⁵⁄₁₆)

77.5
3 (¹⁄₁₆)

77.5
(3¹⁄₁₆)

110 (4⁵⁄₁₆)

307 (12)

four holes
3 (⅛) dia csk

110 (4⁵⁄₁₆)

102 (4)

88 (3⅜)

33
(1⁷⁄₁₆)

88.5
(6⁷⁄₁₆)

88.5
(6⁷⁄₁₆)

453 (17¹³⁄₁₆)

Fig 25 Left-hand unit, main roof
showing hanger wall positions

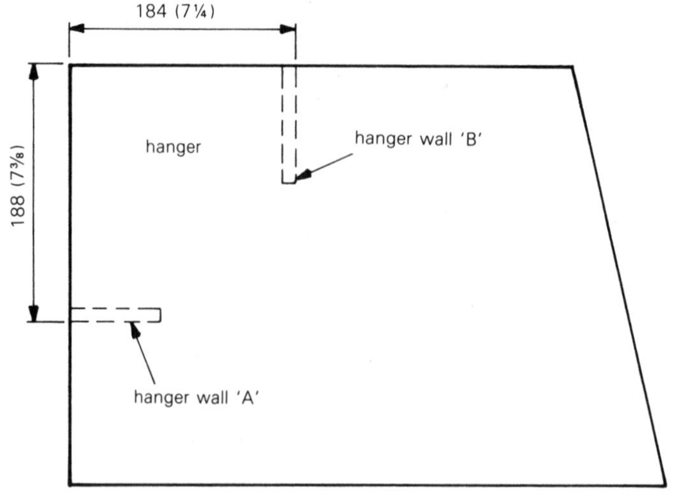
184 (7¼)
188 (7⅜)
hanger
hanger wall 'B'
hanger wall 'A'

Fig 26 Hanger wall 'A'
9 (⅜) thick

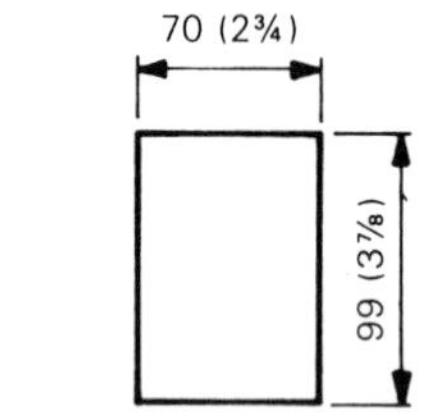
70 (2¾)
99 (3⅞)

Fig 27 Hanger wall 'B'
9 (⅜) thick

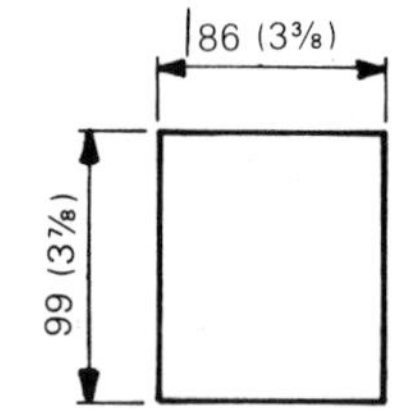
86 (3⅜)
99 (3⅞)

Fig 28 Hanger roof
6 (¼) thick

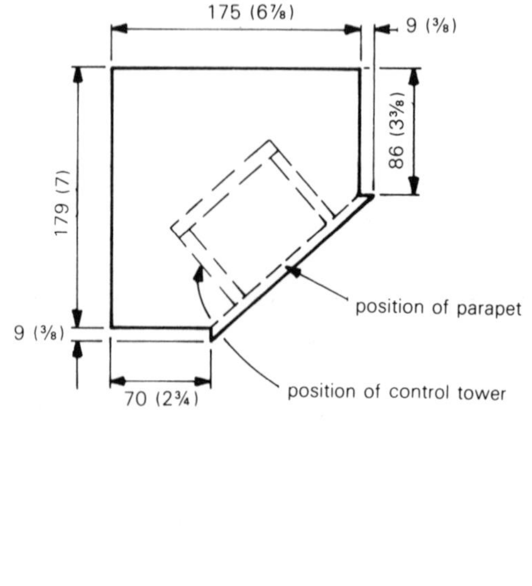
175 (6⅞)
9 (⅜)
86 (3⅜)
179 (7)
9 (⅜)
position of parapet
70 (2¾)
position of control tower

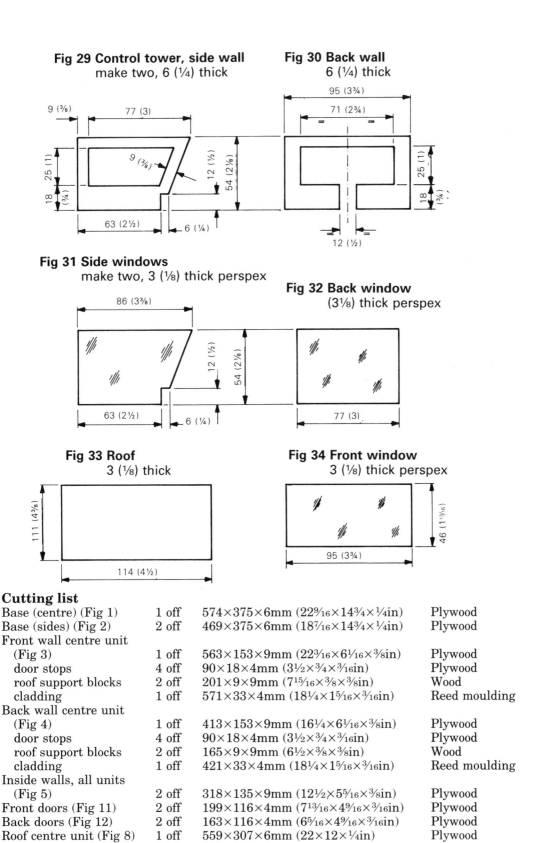

Fig 29 Control tower, side wall
make two, 6 (¼) thick

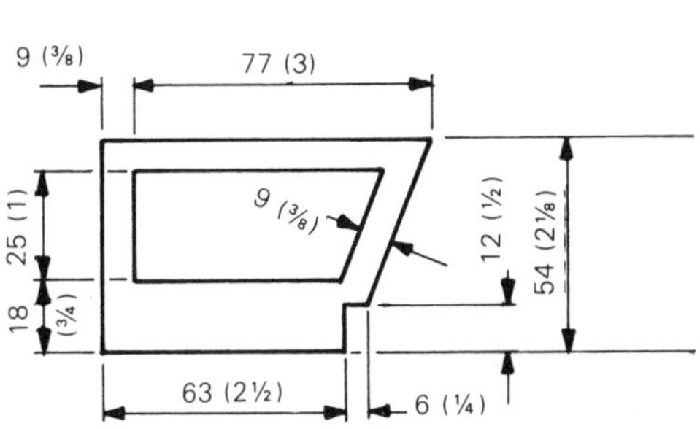
9 (⅜)
77 (3)
9 (⅜)
25 (1)
18 (¾)
12 (½)
54 (2⅛)
63 (2½)
6 (¼)

Fig 30 Back wall
6 (¼) thick

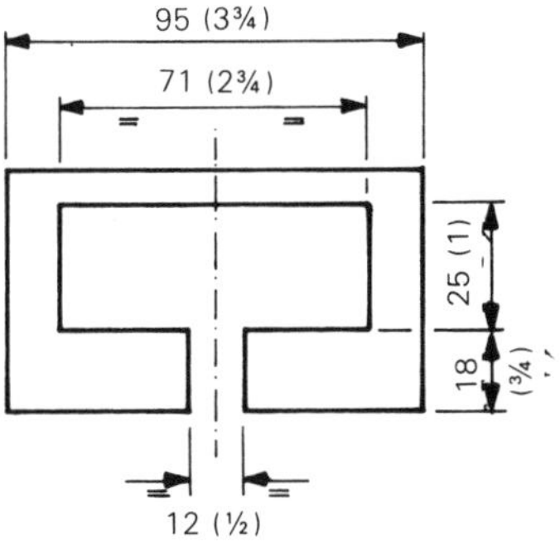
95 (3¾)
71 (2¾)
25 (1)
18 (¾)
12 (½)

Fig 31 Side windows
make two, 3 (⅛) thick perspex

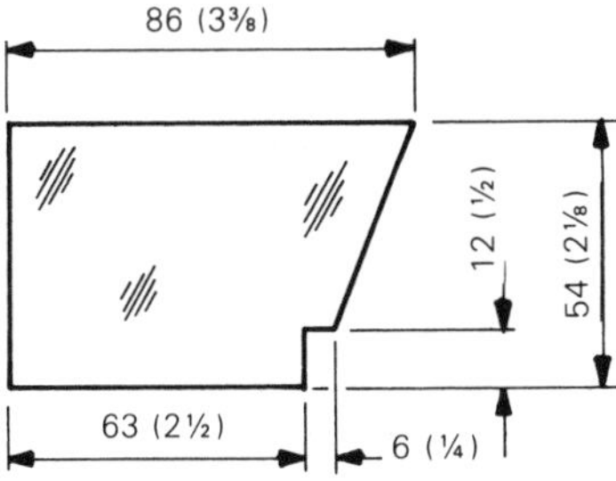
86 (3⅜)
12 (½)
54 (2⅛)
63 (2½)
6 (¼)

Fig 32 Back window
(3⅛) thick perspex

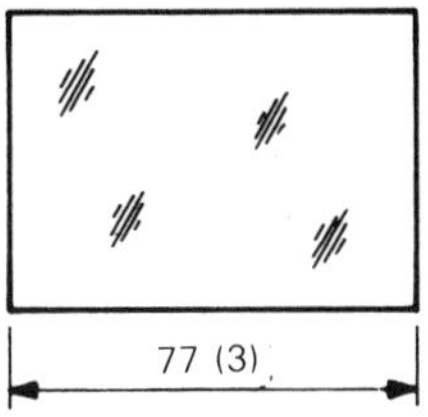
77 (3)

Fig 33 Roof
3 (⅛) thick

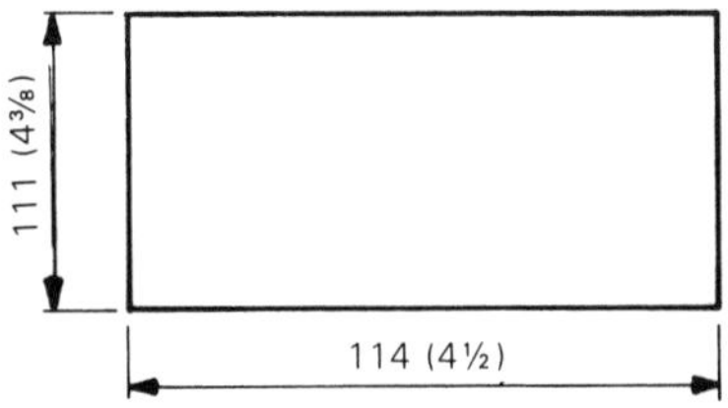
111 (4⅜)
114 (4½)

Fig 34 Front window
3 (⅛) thick perspex

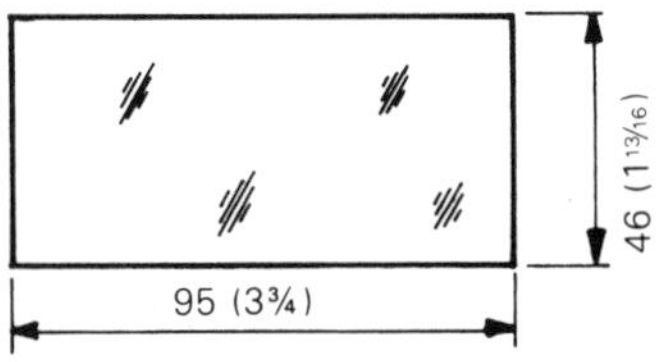
46 (1 13/16)
95 (3¾)

Cutting list

Base (centre) (Fig 1)	1 off	574×375×6mm (22 9/16×14¾×¼in)	Plywood
Base (sides) (Fig 2)	2 off	469×375×6mm (18 7/16×14¾×¼in)	Plywood
Front wall centre unit			
(Fig 3)	1 off	563×153×9mm (22 3/16×6 1/16×⅜in)	Plywood
door stops	4 off	90×18×4mm (3½×¾×3/16in)	Plywood
roof support blocks	2 off	201×9×9mm (7 15/16×⅜×⅜in)	Wood
cladding	1 off	571×33×4mm (18¼×1 5/16×3/16in)	Reed moulding
Back wall centre unit			
(Fig 4)	1 off	413×153×9mm (16¼×6 1/16×⅜in)	Plywood
door stops	4 off	90×18×4mm (3½×¾×3/16in)	Plywood
roof support blocks	2 off	165×9×9mm (6½×⅜×⅜in)	Wood
cladding	1 off	421×33×4mm (18¼×1 5/16×3/16in)	Reed moulding
Inside walls, all units			
(Fig 5)	2 off	318×135×9mm (12½×5 5/16×⅜in)	Plywood
Front doors (Fig 11)	2 off	199×116×4mm (7 13/16×4 9/16×3/16in)	Plywood
Back doors (Fig 12)	2 off	163×116×4mm (6 5/16×4 9/16×3/16in)	Plywood
Roof centre unit (Fig 8)	1 off	559×307×6mm (22×12×¼in)	Plywood

Door guides (Fig 6)	24 off	$107\times9\times9$mm ($4\frac{3}{16}\times\frac{3}{8}\times\frac{3}{8}$in)	Wood
	24 off	$107\times24\times9$mm ($4\frac{3}{16}\times\frac{29}{32}\times\frac{3}{8}$in)	Wood
	24 off	$107\times37\times4$mm ($4\frac{3}{16}\times1\frac{15}{32}\times\frac{3}{16}$in)	Plywood
Guide stops (Fig 6)	24 off	$38\times37\times4$mm ($1\frac{1}{2}\times1\frac{15}{16}\times\frac{3}{16}$in)	Plywood
Door runners (Fig 9)	24 off	$25\times12\times12$mm ($1\times\frac{1}{2}\times\frac{1}{2}$in)	Wood
Front walls, side units (Fig 13)	2 off	$464\times153\times9$mm ($18\frac{1}{4}\times6\frac{1}{16}\times\frac{3}{8}$in)	Plywood
door stops	8 off	$90\times18\times4$mm ($3\frac{1}{2}\times\frac{3}{4}\times\frac{3}{16}$in)	Plywood
roof support blocks	4 off	$177\times9\times9$mm ($6\frac{7}{8}\times\frac{3}{8}\times\frac{3}{8}$in)	Wood
cladding	2 off	$472\times33\times4$mm ($18\frac{7}{8}\times1\frac{5}{16}\times\frac{3}{16}$in)	Reed moulding
Back wall, right-hand side unit (Fig 14)	1 off	$389\times153\times9$mm ($15\frac{5}{16}\times6\frac{1}{16}\times\frac{3}{8}$in)	Plywood
door stops	4 off	$90\times18\times4$mm ($3\frac{1}{2}\times\frac{3}{4}\times\frac{3}{16}$in)	Plywood
roof support blocks	2 off	$155\times9\times9$mm ($6\frac{1}{8}\times\frac{3}{8}\times\frac{3}{8}$in)	Wood
cladding	1 off	$389\times33\times4$mm ($15\frac{5}{16}\times1\frac{5}{16}\times\frac{3}{16}$in)	Reed moulding
Outside wall, right-hand side unit (Fig 15)	1 off	$307\times327\times9$mm ($12\times12\frac{15}{16}\times\frac{3}{8}$in)	Plywood
roof support block	1 off	$93\times9\times9$mm ($3\frac{5}{8}\times\frac{3}{8}\times\frac{3}{8}$in)	Wood
cladding	2 off	$120\times22\times4$mm ($4\frac{1}{2}\times1\frac{5}{16}\times\frac{3}{16}$in)	Reed moulding
Training tower side wall (Fig 16)	1 off	$112\times186\times9$mm ($4\frac{1}{2}\times7\frac{3}{8}\times\frac{3}{8}$in)	Plywood
floors (Fig 18)	2 off	$94\times94\times9$mm ($3\frac{3}{4}\times3\frac{3}{4}\times\frac{1}{4}$in)	Plywood
cross beams (Fig 17)	4 off	$112\times22\times9$mm ($4\frac{1}{2}\times\frac{7}{8}\times\frac{3}{8}$in)	Plywood
cladding	6 off	$120\times22\times4$mm ($4\frac{1}{2}\times\frac{7}{8}\times\frac{3}{16}$in)	Reed moulding
Roof, right-hand side unit (Fig 19)	2 off	$453\times307\times6$mm ($17\frac{13}{16}\times12\times\frac{1}{4}$in)	Plywood
Back doors, side units (Fig 20)	4 off	$153\times116\times4$mm ($6\frac{1}{16}\times4\frac{9}{16}\times\frac{3}{16}$in)	Plywood
Front doors, side units (Fig 21)	4 off	$175\times116\times4$mm ($6\frac{13}{16}\times4\frac{9}{16}\times\frac{3}{16}$in)	Plywood
Outside wall, left-hand side unit (Fig 22)	1 off	$307\times240\times9$mm ($12\times9\frac{7}{16}\times\frac{3}{8}$in)	Plywood
roof support block	1 off	$93\times9\times9$mm ($3\frac{5}{8}\times\frac{3}{8}\times\frac{3}{8}$in)	Wood
roof support block	1 off	$179\times9\times9$mm ($7\times\frac{3}{8}\times\frac{3}{8}$in)	Wood
Back wall, left-hand side unit (Fig 23)	1 off	$389\times240\times9$mm ($15\frac{5}{16}\times9\frac{7}{16}\times\frac{3}{8}$in)	Plywood
door stops	4 off	$90\times18\times4$mm ($3\frac{1}{2}\times\frac{3}{4}\times\frac{3}{16}$in)	Plywood
roof support blocks	2 off	$155\times9\times9$mm ($6\frac{1}{8}\times\frac{3}{8}\times\frac{3}{8}$in)	Wood
	1 off	$166\times9\times9$mm ($6\frac{1}{2}\times\frac{3}{8}\times\frac{3}{8}$in)	Wood
cladding	1 off	$389\times33\times4$mm ($15\frac{5}{16}\times1\frac{5}{16}\times\frac{3}{16}$in)	Reed moulding
Roof, left-hand side unit (Fig 24)	1 off	$453\times307\times6$mm ($17\frac{13}{16}\times12\times\frac{3}{16}$in)	Plywood
Hangar wall 'A' (Fig 26)	1 off	$99\times70\times9$mm ($3\frac{7}{8}\times2\frac{3}{4}\times\frac{3}{8}$in)	Plywood
Hangar wall 'B' (Fig 27)	1 off	$99\times86\times9$mm ($3\frac{7}{8}\times3\frac{3}{8}\times\frac{3}{8}$in)	Plywood
Hangar roof (Fig 28)	1 off	$175\times179\times6$mm ($6\frac{7}{8}\times7\times\frac{1}{4}$in)	Plywood
Hangar roof parapet (Fig 28)	1 off	$154\times12\times9$mm ($6\frac{1}{16}\times\frac{1}{2}\times\frac{3}{8}$in)	Plywood
Door rests (Fig 10)	12 off	$38\times20\times15$mm ($1\frac{1}{2}\times\frac{27}{32}\times\frac{5}{8}$in)	Wood
	12 off	$63\times25\times3$mm ($2\frac{1}{2}\times1\times\frac{1}{8}$in)	Plywood

Ancillaries

Door runners (Fig 6)	24 off	18mm ($\frac{3}{4}$in) long×4mm ($\frac{3}{16}$in) dia steel rod	
Control tower, side windows (Fig 31)	2 off	$86\times54\times3$mm ($3\frac{3}{8}\times2\frac{1}{8}\times\frac{1}{8}$in)	Perspex
back window (Fig 32)	1 off	$77\times54\times3$mm ($3\times2\frac{1}{8}\times\frac{1}{8}$in)	Perspex
front window (Fig 34)	1 off	$95\times46\times3$mm ($3\frac{3}{4}\times1\frac{13}{16}\times\frac{1}{8}$in)	Perspex

DOLL'S BUGGY

Designing and building this buggy was a matter of necessity for me, as my daughters had wrecked more than their fair share of commercial buggies and still wanted yet another. This time, though, it is one which should stand up to them.

The buggy itself is simple enough in its construction, but care and thought must be exercised when marking out.

1 As will be seen from the drawings (Fig 2), not all radii have their centres dimensioned. This is not necessary as these can be arrived at by bisecting the finished angle.

2 *Bisecting an angle* (Fig 1)
   a) Lines AB and AC include the angle to be bisected.
   b) Set your compass to any length and

Fig 1 Bisecting an angle

Fig 2 make two, 9 (⅜) thick

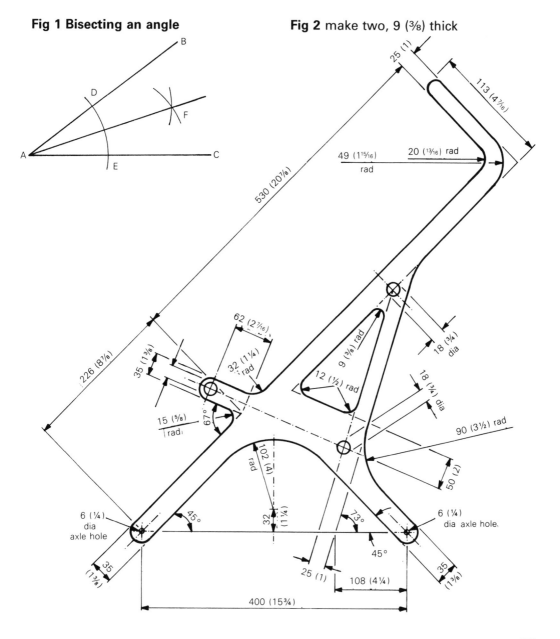

scribe arc DE, using point A as its centre.

c) With your compass at the same setting, draw two more arcs, using points D and E as their centres. These two arcs will then intersect at point F.

d) Draw a line from point A through point F. This resultant line is the centre line for any radius drawn inside lines AB and AC.

3 The first line to be drawn when marking out is a straight horizontal line of 400mm (15¾in) which passes through the centres of the two 6mm (¼in) dia axle holes (Fig 2). This line is the point of reference for *all* other marking out.

4 When the first side has been marked, cut out and smoothed off, use it as a template for marking out the remaining side.

5 Make the material seat as follows:

a) With the material wrong side up, mark a line 12mm (½in) parallel to each edge.

b) Fold each edge on the line you have just drawn, and sew a seam.

c) Turn the top and bottom edge in 50mm (2in), and sew a seam.

6 Cut the three 18mm (¾in) dia dowels to length and glue them in position in one side part only.

7 Slip the material sleeve over the front dowel, behind the lower dowel and over the top dowel.

8 Slide the material away from the dowel ends and glue the remaining side part in position.

9 Cut the axles to length and fit the wheels.

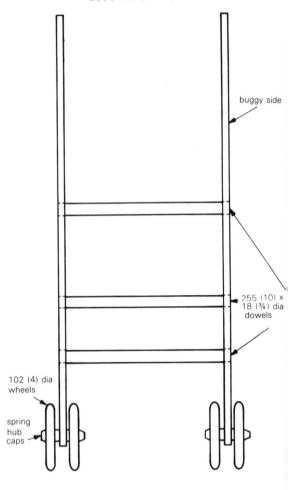

Fig 3 Doll's Buggy
assembled front view

buggy side

255 (10) x 18 (¾) dia dowels

102 (4) dia wheels

spring hub caps

Cutting list

Sides (Fig 2)	2 off	make from 584×672×12mm (23×26½×½in) Plywood
	3 off	255mm (10in) long×18mm (¾in) dia dowel

Ancillaries

Axles	4 off	76mm (3in) long×6mm (¼in) dia steel rod
Spring hub caps	8 off	suitable for 6mm (¼in) dia rod
Wheels (Fig 3)	8 off	102mm (4in) diameter (axle size 6mm (¼in))
Material seat		673mm(26½in) long×280mm (11in) wide

HOBBY HORSE

The hobby horse has been a traditional children's toy for hundreds of years, and when my wife suggested I should include one in this book I didn't think that the children of today would be interested in hobby horses; how wrong I was.

From the moment the horse's head started to take shape, my younger daughter Rachel had already decided it was her 'horsey', it should be red, and daddy wasn't working fast enough to get it finished. In the end, two hobby horses

Fig 1 Head

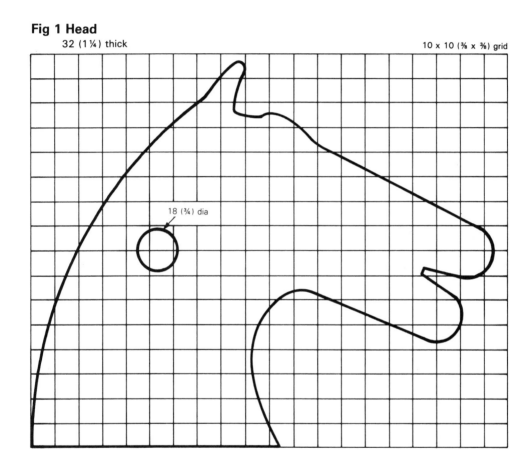

32 (1¼) thick

10 x 10 (⅜ x ⅜) grid

18 (¾) dia

Fig 2 Head plan view
showing mane-locating holes

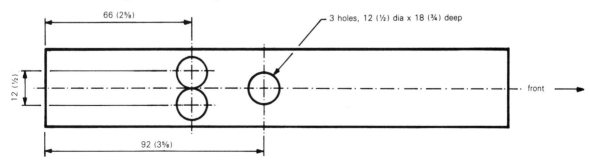

66 (2⅝)

3 holes, 12 (½) dia x 18 (¾) deep

12 (½)

front

92 (3⅝)

Fig 3 Body

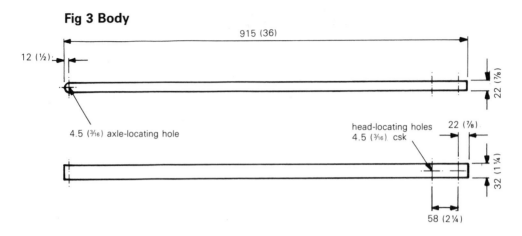

915 (36)

12 (½)

4.5 (³⁄₁₆) axle-locating hole

22 (⅞)

head-locating holes 22 (⅞)
4.5 (³⁄₁₆) csk

32 (1¼)

58 (2¼)

had to be made, one for each daughter.

Because of the rough service a hobby horse is likely to get, this project should be made using hardwood such as beech.

1 Using a grid, draw the head (Fig 1) onto tracing paper and then transpose it onto your work piece.
2 Drill the 18mm (¾in) diameter handle-locating hole (Fig 1), then cut out the head.
3 Drill the three 12mm (½in) diameter mane-locating holes (Fig 2).
4 Cut to size the body, and drill the head- and axle-locating holes (Fig 3).
5 Place the head in position on the body over the head-locating holes. Insert the head-retaining screws into the head-locating holes and gently tap the screws against the underside of the head. Remove the head and drill two pilot holes

into it using the screw marks as centres.
6 Cut to length the handle and insert it into the head.
7 Cut to length the axle and insert it into the body.
8 Screw and glue the head and body together. Wipe away any excess glue and smooth all edges.
9 Complete painting before fixing the mane.
10 Fray the rope, leaving 18mm (¾in) intact for insertion into the mane-locating holes. Then glue the mane into position using contact adhesive. The shortest length of rope is the forelock, and this is inserted into the front mane-locating hole.
11 When fitting the wheels, place flat washers between the body and the wheels.

Cutting list

Head (Fig 1)		make from 195×157×32mm	
		(7¹¹⁄₁₆×6³⁄₁₆×1¼in)	Beechwood
Handle	1 off	193mm (7⅝in) long×18mm (¾in) diameter dowel	
Body (Fig 2)	1 off	915×32×22mm (36×1¼×⅞in)	Beechwood

Ancillaries

Axle	1 off	80mm (3⅛in) long×4mm (³⁄₁₆in) dia steel rod	
Wheels	2 off	76mm (3in) dia (axle dia 4mm (³⁄₁₆in))	
Flat washers	2 off	inside dia 4mm (³⁄₁₆in)	
Spring hub caps	6 off	to suit 4mm (³⁄₁₆in) dia axle	
Screws	2 off	No 10×32mm (1¼in) long	Bright zinc
Mane	2 off	178mm (7in) long×12mm (½in) dia rope	
	1 off	90mm (3½in) long×12mm (½in) dia rope	

SPACE PORT NASUS 5

Space travel is almost an everyday occurrence now, and children accept the realities and possibilities of space and interplanetary travel as readily as children who only a few years ago accepted intercontinental jet aeroplane travel as the way of the future.

When my wife bought my son Peter his first Starcom toy, I was so impressed with the product that I decided to design and build the following project for him to use with his space toys.

Because all parts of this project are individual and will link up with each other, the final scenario for your child's Space Port Nasus 5 can vary each time it is used. If my son and his friends are anything to go by, this will be all day and every day until space, the final frontier, has been crossed.

As many, or as few of the various models included in Nasus 5 can be made as required, and even the bad guys could have a base of their own. All sorts of extra detailing can make this project more interesting for the young space explorer (see colour photo pages 78–9) such as water slide decals (transfers) left over from old plastic model kits, coloured lining tape, and signs cut from magazines etc to add a touch of realism.

Simple, but very effective contours can be achieved on your model by using small pieces of scrap wood etc of various shapes, glued in haphazard locations and painted different colours.

Fig 1 Assembled base plan

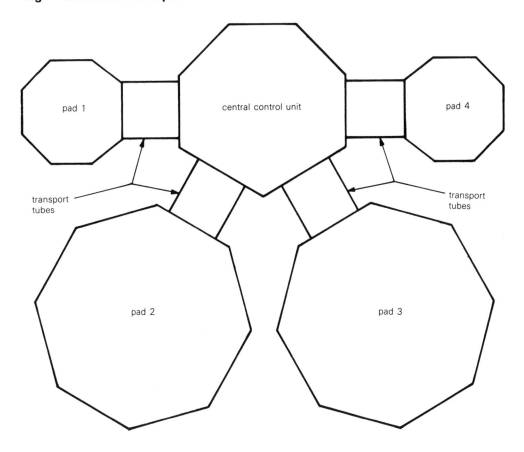

Fig 2 Assembled landing pads 2 and 3

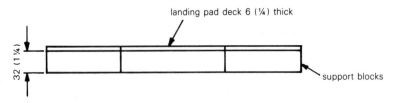

landing pad deck 6 (¼) thick

32 (1¼)

support blocks

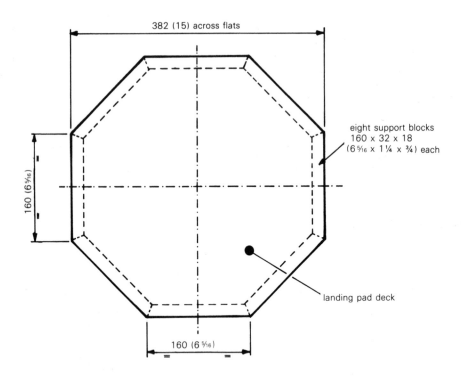

382 (15) across flats

160 (6⁵⁄₁₆)

eight support blocks
160 x 32 x 18
(6⁵⁄₁₆ x 1¼ x ¾) each

landing pad deck

160 (6⁵⁄₁₆)

Fig 3 Assembled landing pads 1 and 4   Plan view

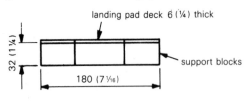

landing pad deck 6 (¼) thick

32 (1¼)

support blocks

180 (7¹⁄₁₆)

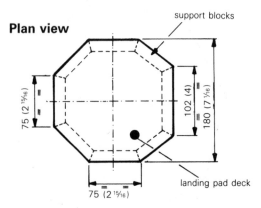

support blocks

75 (2¹⁵⁄₁₆)

102 (4)

180 (7¹⁄₁₆)

landing pad deck

75 (2¹⁵⁄₁₆)

Fig 4 Assembled central control unit

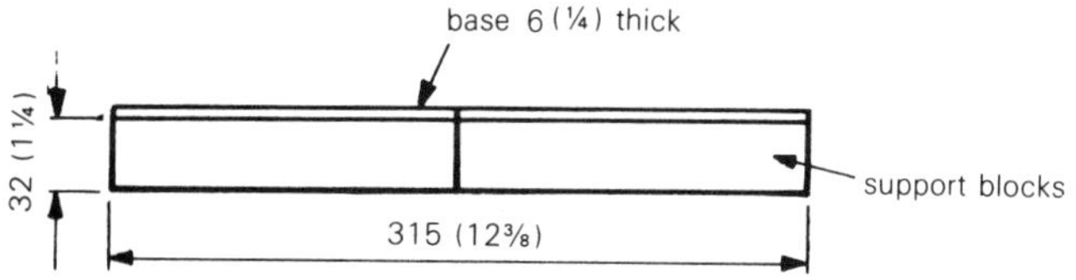

base 6 (¼) thick

support blocks

32 (1¼)

315 (12⅜)

Fig 5 Windows
make five, 1 (¹⁄₁₆) thick

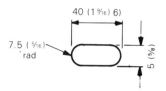

40 (1 ⁹⁄₁₆) 6)

7.5 (⁵⁄₁₆)
rad

5 (⁵⁄₈)

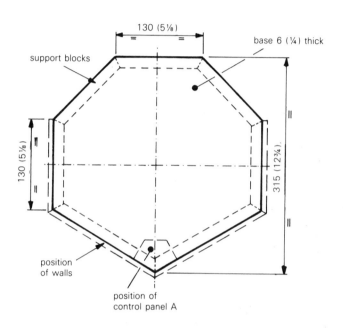

130 (5⅛)

support blocks

base 6 (¼) thick

130 (5⅛)

315 (12¾)

position
of walls

position of
control panel A

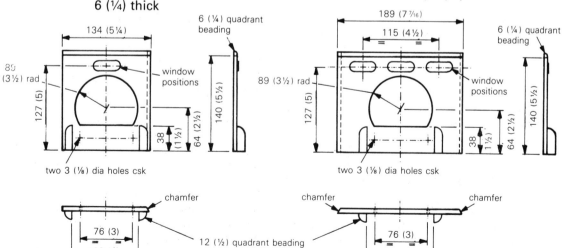

Fig 6 Central control unit side wall
make one of each hand,
6 (¼) thick

6 (¼) quadrant
beading

134 (5¼)

89
(3½) rad

window
positions

127 (5)

140 (5½)

38
(1½)

64 (2½)

two 3 (⅛) dia holes csk

chamfer

76 (3)

102 (4)

12 (½) quadrant beading

Fig 7 Central control unit front wall
make two, 6 (¼) thick

189 (7⁷⁄₁₆)

115 (4½)

6 (¼) quadrant
beading

89 (3½) rad

window
positions

127 (5)

140 (5½)

38
1½

64 (2½)

two 3 (⅛) dia holes csk

chamfer

chamfer

76 (3)

102 (4)

61

Fig 8 Control panel A wall panel
make one of each hand

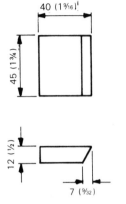

40 (1 9/16)
45 (1 3/4)
12 (1/2)
7 (9/32)

Fig 9 Control desk A desk unit
18 (3/4) thick

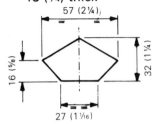

57 (2 1/4)
16 (5/8)
32 (1 1/4)
27 (1 1/16)

Fig 10 Assembled desk unit

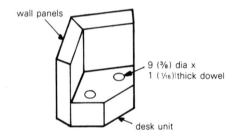

wall panels

9 (3/8) dia x
1 (1/16) thick dowel

desk unit

1 Landing pads 1–4 and the central control unit are marked out inside circles of shown diameter. Note, not all sides of these parts are equal.

2 Mitre *all* landing pad support blocks when cutting them to length. The correct mitre angle can be found by bisecting the angle at each corner (see Doll's Buggy, page 16 step 2, for an example of bisecting an angle).

3 Mark, cut out and assemble landing pads 2 and 3 (Fig 2), 1 and 4 (Fig 3) and the central control unit base (Fig 4).

4 To enable the central control unit side walls (Figs 6 and 7) to fit neatly together, chamfer each adjoining wall edge gradually. Dry assemble walls before screwing and glueing in position.

5 Cut quadrant beading to length, shape as shown (Figs 6 and 7), and glue in position. Also at this stage, cut out and glue the simulated windows (Fig 5) in position (see Figs 6 and 7).

6 Assemble control panel A (Figs 8, 9 and 10), and glue it in position inside the central control unit (Fig 4).

7 Cut out de-contamination unit base (Fig 11), wall A (Fig 12), wall D (Fig 13), wall C (Fig 14), wall B (Fig 15) and wall E (Fig 16).

8 Cut to length the reed moulding (Figs 17 and 18) and their respective nozzles. Drill nozzle holes. Enlarge the nozzle holes slightly so that the nozzles do not split the reed moulding when inserted.

Reed moulding is used in the construction of the de-contamination unit to represent overhead pipe work which would probably be present if such a real building existed.

9 Assemble de-contamination unit walls to base as shown in Fig 11. Chamfer wall edges to fit as necessary. Use 6mm (1/4in) quadrant moulding as corner blocks inside and outside the de-contamination unit.

Fig 11 De-contamination unit base showing wall positions
6 (¼) thick

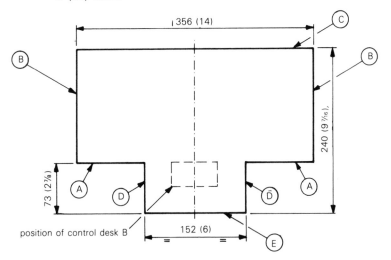

Fig 12 Wall A
make one of each hand, 6 (¼) thick

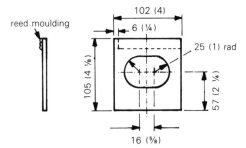

Fig 13 Wall D
make two, 6 (¼) thick

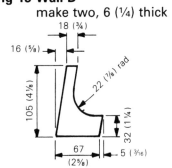

10 Control desk B (Fig 19) can now be cut out, assembled and glued in position.

11 Cut to size, shape and assemble steps (Fig 20). Any number of step units can be made as required.

12 Cut out Big Ears tracking station base (Fig 21), front wall (Fig 22), inside wall (Fig 23), right-hand side wall (Fig 24), left-hand side wall (Fig 25) and back wall (Fig 26).

13 Assemble Big Ears walls as shown in Fig 21.

14 Shape control panel (Fig 28) and glue in position (Fig 21).

15 Mark, cut out and drill radar arm (Fig 29).

16 Cut out radar arm base (Fig 30) and glue to radar arm (Fig 29).

17 Place assembled radar arm on tracking station roof, and screw arm in position through roof (Fig 27).

18 Use plastic pipe, 54mm (2⅛in) outside diameter to make the radar dish (Fig 31). Screw, and epoxy glue dish in position on top of radar arm.

19 Glue tracking station roof with assembled radar arm to previously assembled Big Ears walls.

20 Any quantity of ramps (Fig 32) can be made as required.

21 Before making any transport tubes (Fig 33), cut out a card template (Fig 34). Do not cut tubes to length until angled section has been removed.

22 Secure transport tube pipe firmly. Wrap the card template around the pipe,

Fig 14 Wall C
make two, 6 (¼) thick

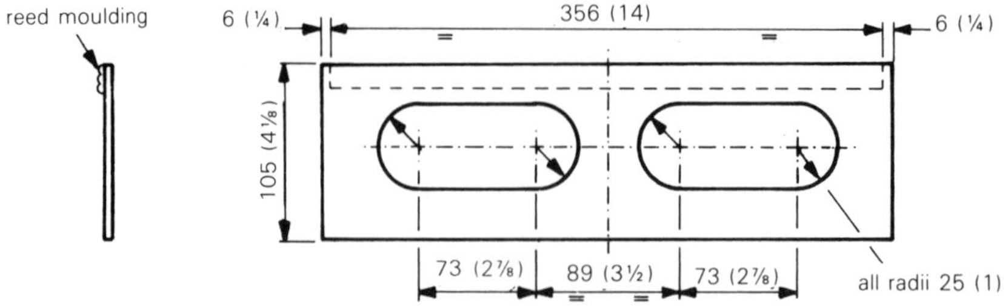
reed moulding
6 (¼)
356 (14)
6 (¼)
105 (4⅛)
73 (2⅞)
89 (3½)
73 (2⅞)
all radii 25 (1)

Fig 15 Wall B
make two, 6 (¼) thick

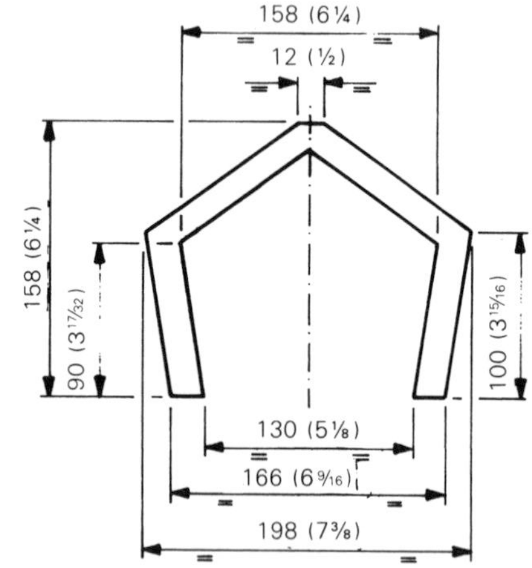
158 (6¼)
12 (½)
158 (6¼)
90 (3¹⁷⁄₃₂)
100 (3¹⁵⁄₁₆)
130 (5⅛)
166 (6⁹⁄₁₆)
198 (7⅞)

Fig 16 Wall E
6 (¼) thick

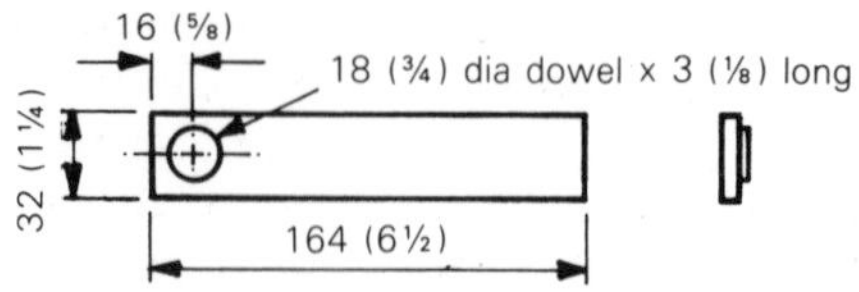
16 (⅝)
18 (¾) dia dowel x 3 (⅛) long
32 (1¼)
164 (6½)

Fig 17 Wall A
reed moulding nozzle positions

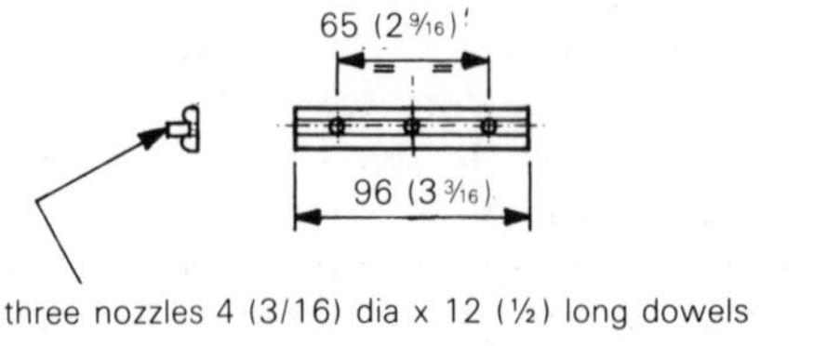
65 (2⁹⁄₁₆)
96 (3³⁄₁₆)
three nozzles 4 (3/16) dia x 12 (½) long dowels

Fig 18 Wall C
reed moulding nozzle positions

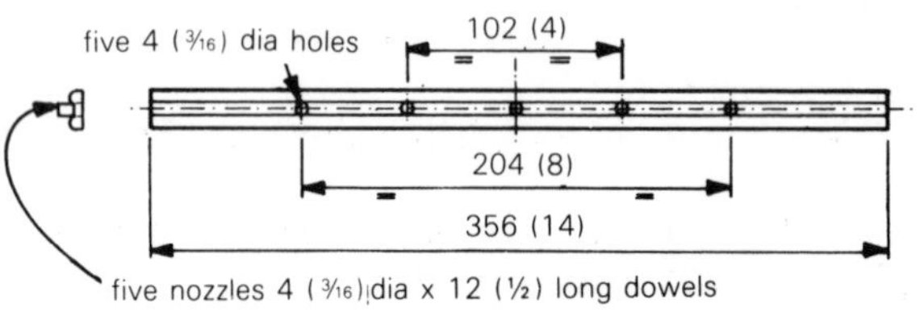
five 4 (³⁄₁₆) dia holes
102 (4)
204 (8)
356 (14)
five nozzles 4 (³⁄₁₆) dia x 12 (½) long dowels

Fig 19 Assembled view of control desk B

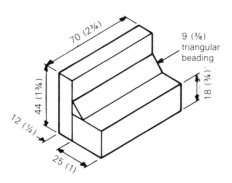

70 (2¾)
9 (⅜) triangular beading
44 (1¾)
18 (¾)
12 (½)
25 (1)

Fig 20 Assembled view of steps
each step 12.6 (½) thick

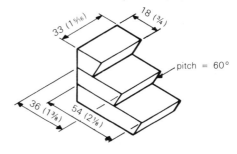

33 (1⁵⁄₁₆)
18 (¾)
pitch = 60°
36 (1⅜)
54 (2⅛)

Fig 21 Big Ears tracking station, base
6 (¼) thick

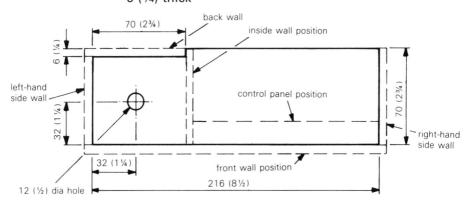

70 (2¾)
back wall
inside wall position
6 (¼)
left-hand side wall
control panel position
32 (1¼)
70 (2¾)
right-hand side wall
32 (1¼)
front wall position
12 (½) dia hole
216 (8½)

Fig 22 Front wall
6 (¼) thick

position of 6 (¼) x 6 (¼) quadrant moulding

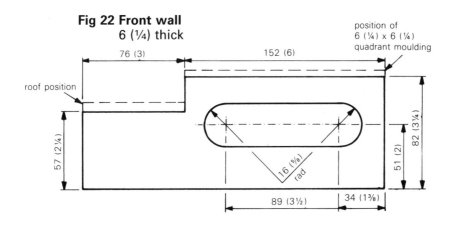

76 (3)
152 (6)
roof position
57 (2¼)
82 (3¼)
16 (⁵⁄₈) rad
51 (2)
89 (3½)
34 (1⅜)

65

Fig 23 Inside wall
6 (¼) thick

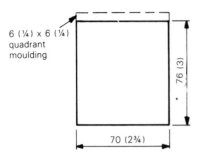

6 (¼) x 6 (¼) quadrant moulding

76 (3)

70 (2¾)

Fig 24 Right-hand side wall
Big Ears tracking station 6 (¼) thick

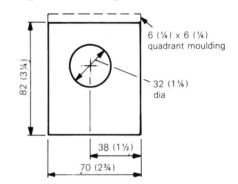

6 (¼) x 6 (¼) quadrant moulding

32 (1¼) dia

82 (3¼)

38 (1½)

70 (2¾)

Fig 25 Left-hand side wall
6 (¼) thick

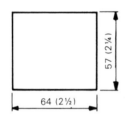

57 (2¼)

64 (2½)

Fig 26 Back wall
6 (¼) thick

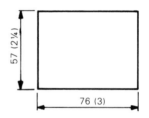

57 (2¼)

76 (3)

Fig 27 Roof
6 (¼) thick

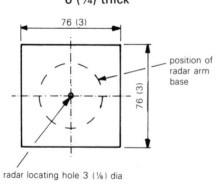

76 (3)

76 (3)

position of radar arm base

radar locating hole 3 (⅛) dia

Fig 28 Control panel
18 (¾) thick

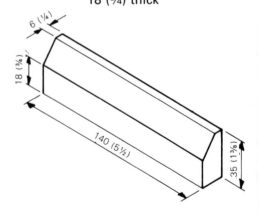

6 (¼)

18 (¾)

140 (5½)

35 (1⅜)

Fig 29 Radar arm
9 (⅜) thick

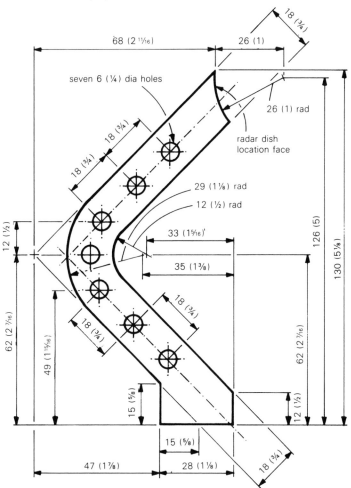

68 (2 ¹¹⁄₁₆)   26 (1)   18 (¾)

seven 6 (¼) dia holes

18 (¾)   18 (¾)   18 (¾)

26 (1) rad

radar dish
location face

29 (1⅛) rad
12 (½) rad

33 (1⁵⁄₁₆)
35 (1⅜)

12 (½)

62 (2 ⁷⁄₁₆)

49 (1¹⁵⁄₁₆)

18 (¾)   18 (¾)

15 (⅝)

126 (5)
130 (5⅛)

62 (2 ⁷⁄₁₆)

12 (½)

15 (⅝)

47 (1⅞)   28 (1⅛)   18 (¾)

Fig 30 Radar arm base
6 (¼) thick

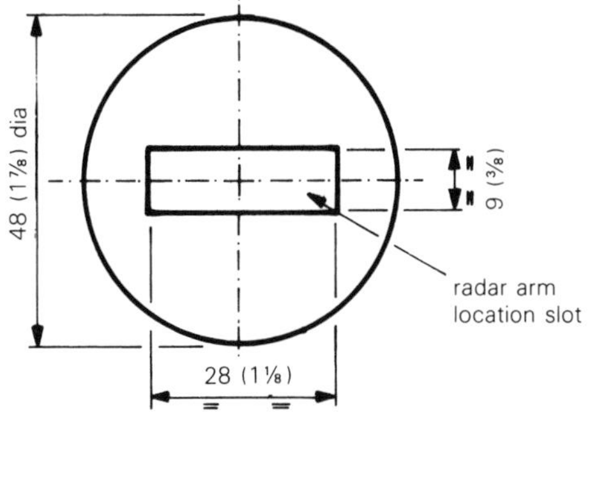

48 (1⅞) dia

9 (⅜)

radar arm
location slot

28 (1⅛)

Fig 31 Radar dish
make from 54 (2⅛) dia plastic pipe

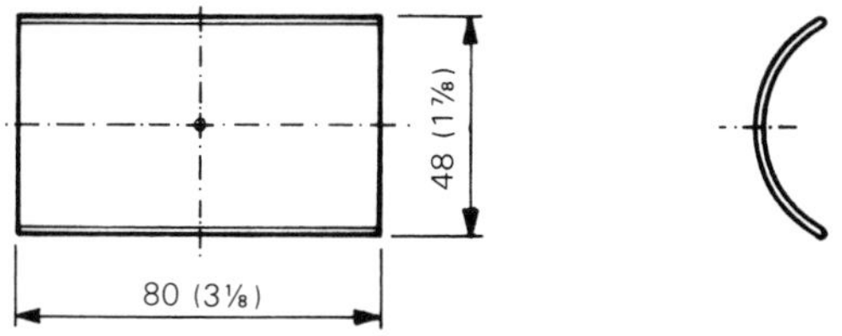

48 (1⅞)

80 (3⅛)

67

Fig 32 Ramp

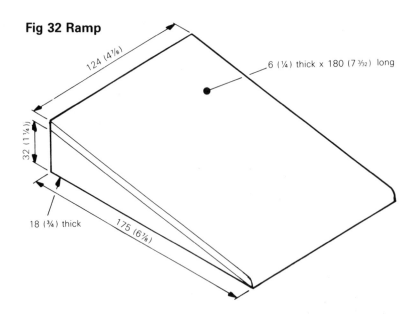

124 (4⅞)

6 (¼) thick x 180 (7 3/32) long

32 (1¼)

18 (¾) thick

175 (6⅞)

95 (3¾) dia plastic pipe

Fig 33 View of assembled transport tube

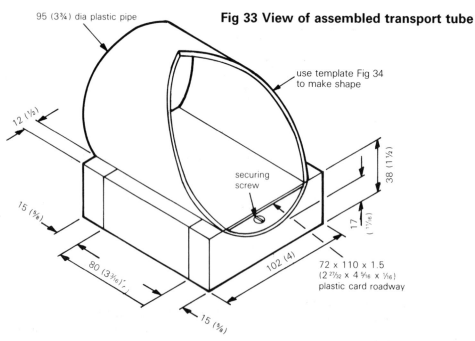

use template Fig 34
to make shape

12 (½)

securing
screw

38 (1½)

15 (⅝)

17
(11/16)

80 (3 3/16)

102 (4)

72 x 110 x 1.5
(2 27/32 x 4 5/16 x 1/16)
plastic card roadway

15 (⅝)

Fig 34 Transport tube cutting template
thick card

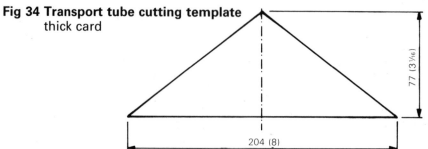

77 (3 1/16)

204 (8)

positioning the longest edge of the template anywhere along the rim of the pipe. Mark around the template, and cut out the resultant shape using a coping saw.

23 Cut out the transport tube support blocks (Fig 33). Use the rim of the pipe as a template to mark its resting position on the front and back blocks.

24 Screw and epoxy glue each transport tube to its front and back support blocks, then glue each side block in position tight against the transport tube sides.

25 Chamfer the sides of the plastic card roadway (Fig 33), and using polystyrene cement, glue it in position.

Cutting list

Landing pads 2 and 3 (Fig 2)
landing pad deck	2 off	$382 \times 382 \times 6$mm ($15 \times 15 \times \frac{1}{4}$in)	Plywood
support blocks	16 off	$160 \times 32 \times 18$mm ($6\frac{5}{16} \times 1\frac{1}{4} \times \frac{3}{4}$in)	Wood

Landing pads 1 and 4 (Fig 3)
landing pad deck	2 off	$180 \times 180 \times 6$mm ($7\frac{1}{16} \times 7\frac{1}{16} \times \frac{1}{4}$in)	Plywood
support blocks	16 off	$75 \times 32 \times 18$mm ($2\frac{15}{16} \times 2\frac{15}{16} \times \frac{1}{4}$in)	Wood

Central control unit
base (Fig 4)	1 off	$315 \times 315 \times 6$mm ($12\frac{3}{4} \times 12\frac{3}{4} \times \frac{1}{4}$in)	Plywood
support blocks	5 off	$130 \times 32 \times 18$mm ($5\frac{1}{8} \times 1\frac{1}{4} \times \frac{3}{4}$in)	Wood
	2 off	$180 \times 32 \times 6$mm ($7\frac{1}{16} \times 1\frac{1}{4} \times \frac{1}{4}$in)	Wood
windows (Fig 5)	5 off	$40 \times 15 \times 1$mm ($1\frac{9}{16} \times \frac{5}{8} \times \frac{1}{16}$in)	Plywood
side walls (Fig 6)	2 off	$134 \times 127 \times 6$mm ($5\frac{1}{4} \times 5 \times \frac{1}{4}$in)	Plywood
	2 off	6mm ($\frac{1}{4}$in) quadrant beading 134mm ($5\frac{1}{4}$in) long	
	4 off	12mm ($\frac{1}{2}$in) quadrant beading 38mm ($1\frac{1}{2}$in) long	
front walls (Fig 7)	2 off	$189 \times 127 \times 6$mm ($7\frac{7}{16} \times 5 \times \frac{1}{4}$in)	Plywood
	2 off	6mm ($\frac{1}{4}$in) quadrant beading 189mm ($7\frac{7}{16}$in) long	
	2 off	12mm ($\frac{1}{2}$in) quadrant beading 38mm ($1\frac{1}{2}$in) long	
control desk B (Fig 19)	1 off	$70 \times 25 \times 18$mm ($2\frac{3}{4} \times 1 \times \frac{3}{4}$in)	Wood
	1 off	$70 \times 44 \times 12$mm ($2\frac{3}{4} \times 1\frac{3}{4} \times \frac{1}{2}$in)	Wood
	1 off	9mm ($\frac{3}{8}$in) $\times$ 70mm ($2\frac{3}{4}$in) triangular beading	
Steps (Fig 20)	1 off	$54 \times 33 \times 12.6$mm ($2\frac{1}{8} \times 1\frac{5}{16} \times \frac{1}{2}$in)	Wood
	1 off	$36 \times 33 \times 12.6$mm ($1\frac{3}{8} \times 1\frac{5}{16} \times \frac{1}{2}$in)	Wood
	1 off	$18 \times 33 \times 12.6$mm ($\frac{3}{4} \times 1\frac{5}{16} \times \frac{1}{2}$in)	Wood

Big Ears tracking station
base (Fig 21)	1 off	$216 \times 70 \times 6$mm ($8\frac{1}{2} \times 2\frac{3}{4} \times \frac{1}{4}$in)	Plywood
front wall (Fig 22)	1 off	$228 \times 82 \times 6$mm ($9 \times 3\frac{1}{4} \times \frac{1}{4}$in)	Plywood
inside wall (Fig 23)	1 off	$70 \times 76 \times 6$mm ($2\frac{3}{4} \times 3 \times \frac{1}{4}$in)	Plywood
side wall (right) (Fig 24)	1 off	$70 \times 82 \times 6$mm ($2\frac{3}{4} \times 3\frac{1}{4} \times \frac{1}{4}$in)	Plywood
side wall (left) (Fig 25)	1 off	$64 \times 57 \times 6$mm ($2\frac{1}{2} \times 2\frac{1}{4} \times \frac{1}{4}$in)	Plywood
back wall (Fig 26)	1 off	$76 \times 57 \times 6$mm ($3 \times 2\frac{1}{4} \times \frac{1}{4}$in)	Plywood
roof (Fig 27)	1 off	$76 \times 76 \times 6$mm ($3 \times 3 \times \frac{1}{4}$in)	Plywood
control panel (Fig 28)	1 off	$140 \times 35 \times 18$mm ($5\frac{1}{2} \times 1\frac{3}{8} \times \frac{3}{4}$in)	Wood
radar arm (Fig 29)		make from $75 \times 130 \times 9$mm ($3 \times 5\frac{1}{8} \times \frac{3}{8}$in)	Plywood
radar arm base (Fig 30)	1 off	48mm ($1\frac{7}{8}$in) dia$\times$6mm ($\frac{1}{4}$in)	Plywood
radar dish (Fig 31)		make from 80mm ($3\frac{1}{8}$in) long$\times$54mm ($2\frac{1}{8}$in) dia plastic pipe	

Ramps (Fig 32)
	2 off	$175 \times 32 \times 18$mm ($6\frac{7}{8} \times 4\frac{7}{8} \times \frac{3}{4}$in)	Wood
	1 off	$124 \times 180 \times 6$mm ($4\frac{7}{8} \times 7\frac{3}{32} \times \frac{1}{4}$in)	Wood

Transport tubes (Fig 33)
tubes	4 off	95mm ($3\frac{3}{4}$in) dia$\times$110mm ($4\frac{7}{16}$in) long plastic pipe	
side blocks	8 off	$80 \times 38 \times 12$mm ($3\frac{3}{16} \times 1\frac{1}{2} \times \frac{1}{2}$in)	Wood
front/back blocks	8 off	$102 \times 38 \times 15$mm ($4 \times 1\frac{1}{2} \times \frac{5}{8}$in)	Wood
tube template (Fig 34)	1 off	204×77mm ($8 \times 3\frac{1}{16}$in)	Card
roadway	4 off	$110 \times 72 \times 1.5$mm ($4\frac{5}{16} \times 2\frac{27}{32} \times \frac{1}{16}$in)	Plastic card

OFF-ROAD RACER

The Off-road Racer project has been designed for use with the Four-wheel-drive Vehicle and Trailer. Together, they make up a complete racing outfit and more than one Off-road Racer can be made for races between friends.

Hardwood has again been used for this project because of its durability and appearance, but any wood will do if hardwood is not available. Sealing the wood is important, and this can either be done with matt varnish or paint. If you choose to paint your Off-road Racer, the use of small stickers and decals (transfers) will add extra interest to your model and give a very realistic appearance. To prolong the life of your transfers, coat them with varnish.

1 As can be seen in Fig 1, the body is shaped from one piece of wood. If you do not have wood the exact thickness, glue a few pieces of wood together until the correct thickness is achieved. This can either be done using wood of the same type and colouring, or using different coloured woods for a natural split colour scheme.

2 Before any shaping is done, mark and cut out the cockpit area. Remove the bulk of waste material using a drill.

3 Cut the two slots at the front of the body (Fig 1). These will house the front wheel assembly (Fig 2).

4 Drill the two 9mm (⅜in) dia×12mm (½in) deep holes either side of the cockpit.

5 Mark the angle of the top face of the

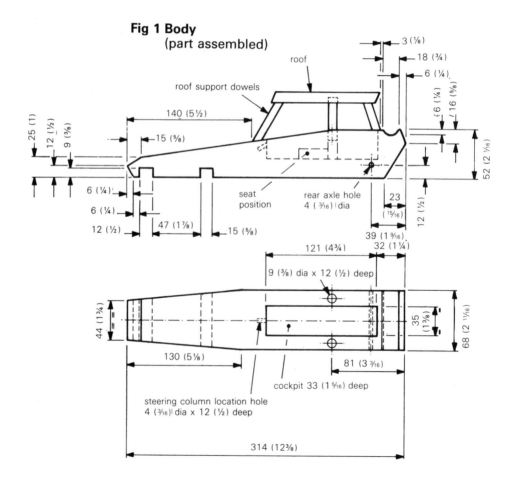

Fig 1 Body
(part assembled)

Fig 2 Front wheel assembly

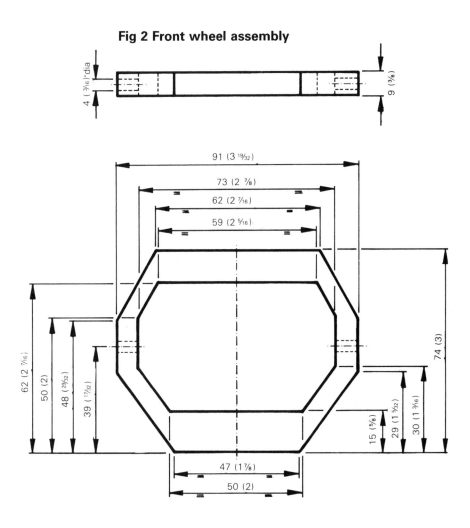

Fig 3 Steering wheel assembly

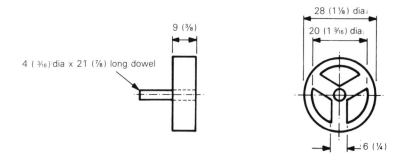

4 (³/₁₆)'dia x 21 (⅞) long dowel

Fig 4 Seat base
12 (½) thick

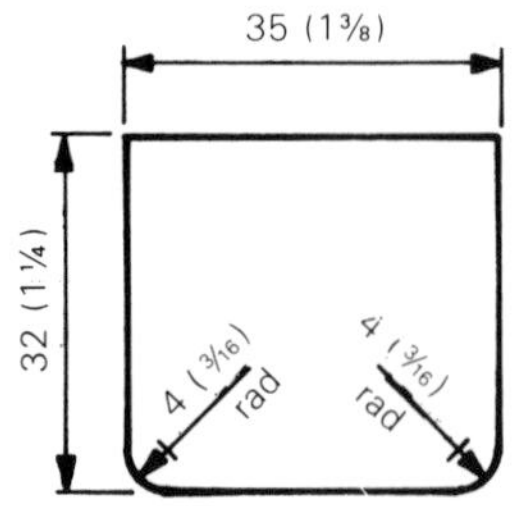

35 (1⅜)

32 (1¼)

4 (3/16) rad

4 (3/16) rad

Fig 5 Seat back

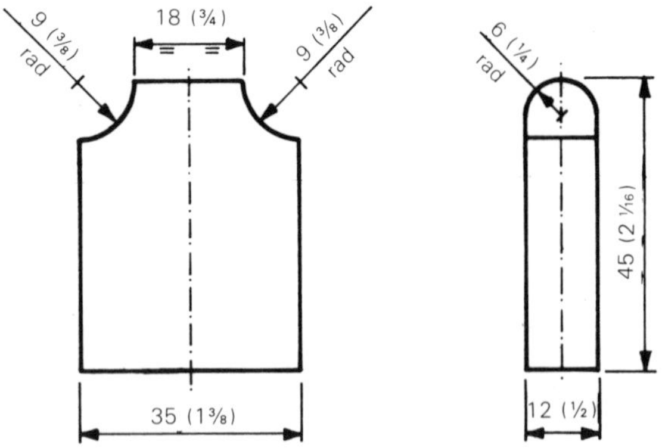

9 (3/8) rad

18 (¾)

9 (3/8) rad

35 (1⅜)

6 (¼) rad

45 (2 1/16)

12 (½)

Fig 6 Roof

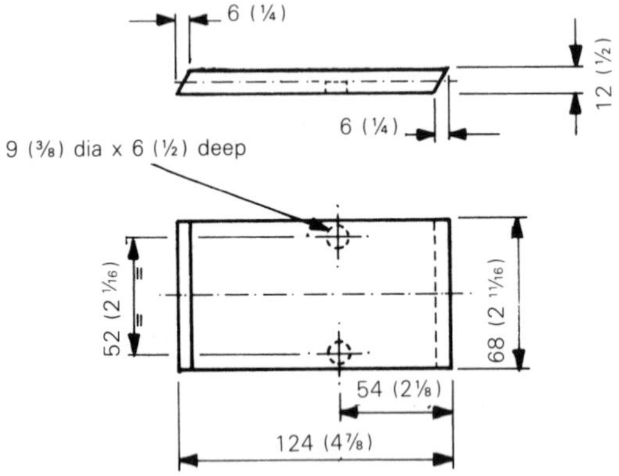

6 (¼)

12 (½)

6 (¼)

9 (3/8) dia x 6 (½) deep

52 (2 1/16)

68 (2 11/16)

54 (2⅛)

124 (4⅞)

Fig 7 Wind break

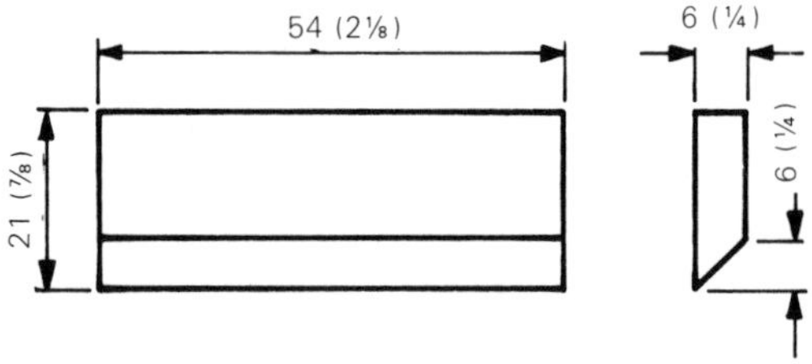

54 (2⅛)

6 (¼)

21 (⅞)

6 (¼)

Fig 8 Side induction pod
(left) make one of each hand

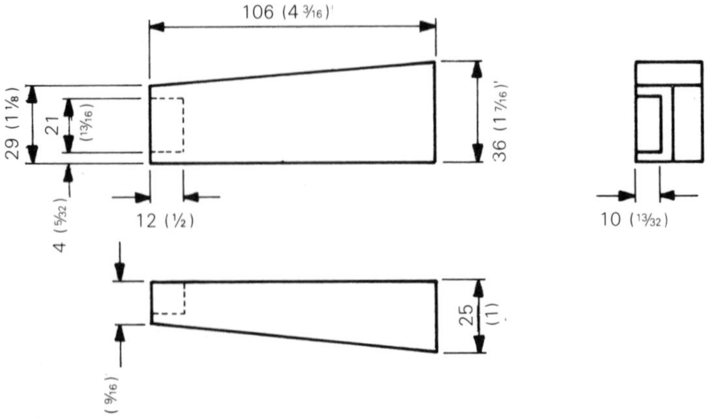

106 (4 3/16)

29 (1⅛)

21 (13/16)

36 (1 7/16)

4 (5/32)

12 (½)

10 (13/32)

14 (9/16)

25 (1)

Fig 9 Wind break and side induction positions

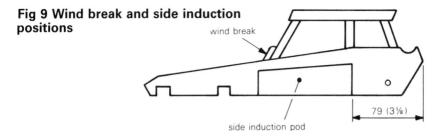

wind break

side induction pod

79 (3⅛)

body, and remove the bulk of the waste wood using a saw. Sand flat using rough abrasive paper and finish using fine abrasive paper.

6 Mark and cut the front and rear body angles.

7 Mark and shape the body sides.

8 Make the half round indentation at the rear of the vehicle using abrasive paper wrapped around a piece of dowelling.

9 Cut out the front wheel assembly (Fig 2) and glue in position.

10 Assemble the steering wheel assembly (Fig 3) and glue in position (see Fig 1).

11 Cut out and shape the seat (Fig 4) and glue in position (see Fig 1).

12 Cut to length the six roof support

dowels (see Cutting List).

13 Glue in position the middle roof support dowels (Fig 1).

14 Locate the roof (Fig 6) onto the centre roof support dowels (see Fig 1). Shape the front and rear roof support dowels to fit comfortably under the roof. Glue dowels and roof in position and finally glue the wind break (Fig 7) in position across the front roof support dowels (see Fig 9).

14 Shape and glue in position the side induction pods (Figs 8 and 9).

15 Cut the front and rear axles to length and fit the wheels. Use one flat washer between each front wheel and front wheel assembly, and five flat washers between each rear wheel and the body.

Cutting list

Body (Fig 1)	1 off	314×68×52mm (12⅜×2¹¹⁄₁₆×2¹⁄₁₆in)	Wood
Front wheel assembly (Fig 2)	1 off	91×74×9mm (3¹⁹⁄₃₂×3×⅜in)	Plywood
Steering wheel (Fig 3)	1 off	28mm (1⅛in) dia×9mm (⅜in) thick	Wood
Steering column (Fig 3)	1 off	21mm (⅞in) long×4mm (³⁄₁₆in) dia dowel	
Seat base (Fig 4)	1 off	35×32×12mm (1⅜×1¼×½in)	Wood
Seat back (Fig 5)	1 off	35×45×12mm (1⅜×2¹⁄₁₆×½in)	Wood
Roof support dowels (Fig 1)			
front	2 off	52mm (2¹⁄₁₆in) long×9mm (⅜in) dia dowel	
middle	2 off	46mm (1¹³⁄₁₆in) long×9mm (⅜in) dia dowel	
rear	2 off	32mm (1¼in) long×9mm (⅜in) dia dowel	
Roof (Fig 6)	1 off	124×68×12mm (4⅞×2¹¹⁄₁₆×½in)	Wood
Wind break (Figs 7 and 9)	1 off	54×21×6mm (2⅛×⅞×¼in)	Wood
Side induction pods (Figs 8–9)	2 off	106×36×25mm (4³⁄₁₆×1⁷⁄₁₆×1in)	Wood

Ancillaries

Rear axle	1 off	155mm (6⅛in) long×4mm (³⁄₁₆in) dia metal rod
Front stub axles	2 off	38mm (1½in) long×4mm (³⁄₁₆in) dia metal rod
Flat washers	12 off	inside diameter 4mm (³⁄₁₆in)
Spring hub caps	6 off	suitable for 4mm (³⁄₁₆in) dia rod
Front wheels	2 off	model aircraft type 62mm (2⁷⁄₁₆in) dia
Rear wheels	2 off	76mm (3in) dia×36mm (1⁷⁄₁₆in) wide

FOUR-WHEEL-DRIVE VEHICLE

The go anywhere, do anything four-wheel-drive vehicle is becoming as popular with the private user as it is with the professional driver. No longer only found up to their axles in mud in the middle of nowhere, these vehicles can often be seen in pristine condition taking pride of place on an owner's driveway.

The old spartan, functional design has given way to one which is both eye catching and comfortable. These vehicles come in all shapes and sizes, and some of the customised models look very impressive indeed with their air-brushed finishes, wide wheels and large bumpers.

The project is not based on any actual model, but has been designed to capture the strength and durability of the modern four-wheel-drive vehicle. Used with the Off-Road Racer (page 70) and the Trailer (page 85), this model will take your child's racing team anywhere.

The prototype has been left in a natural wood finish with a protective coating of matt varnish, but if you have a flair with an air brush, why not try your hand at a bit of customising?

When making this project a lot of parts have to be cut out before they can finally be assembled as a whole. For this reason, do not glue any parts together until instructed to do so and until you are satisfied that they fit together well. It is a good idea to keep all parts awaiting assembly together in a small box.

1 Just like the real thing, this model is built from the ground upwards. Start by marking out the longitudinal chassis members (Fig 1). Ensure that the axle hole centres are marked before any cutting begins.

2 Cut out the front and rear chassis cross members (Figs 2 and 3). Glue them to the

Fig 1 Longitudinal chassis member
make two, 15 (⅝) thick

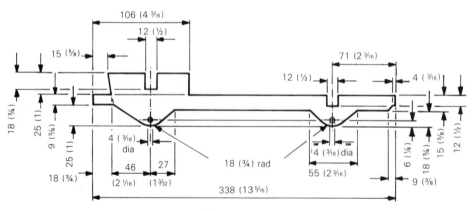

Fig 2 Front cross member
12 (½) thick

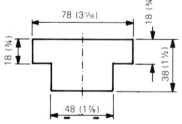

Fig 3 Cross member
12 (½) thick

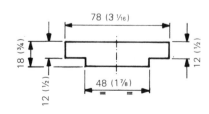

Fig 4 General arrangement of chassis and body parts

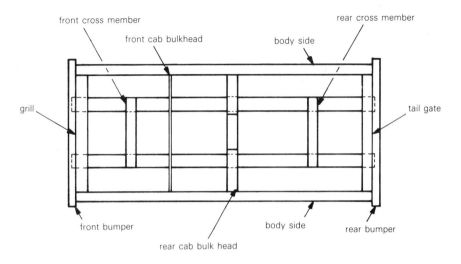

front cross member

rear cross member

front cab bulkhead

body side

grill

tail gate

front bumper

body side

rear bumper

rear cab bulk head

Fig 5 Tail gate
12 (½) thick

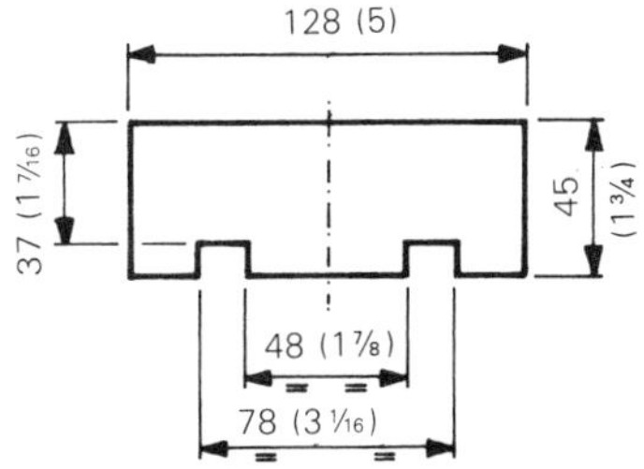

128 (5)

37 (1⁷⁄₁₆)

45 (1¾)

48 (1⅞)

78 (3¹⁄₁₆)

Fig 6 Rear cab bulk head
12 (½) thick

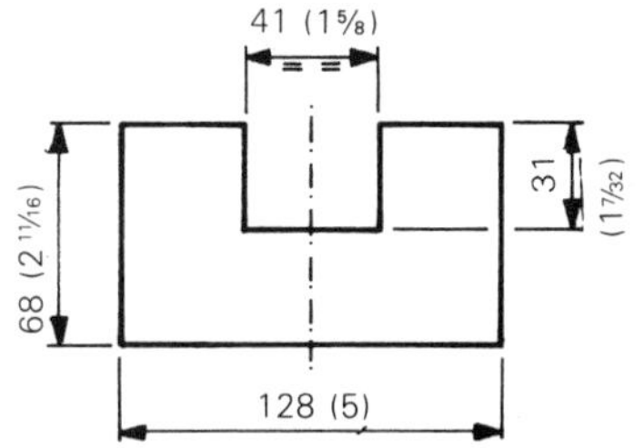

41 (1⅝)

68 (2¹¹⁄₁₆)

31 (1⁷⁄₃₂)

128 (5)

Fig 7 Grill detail

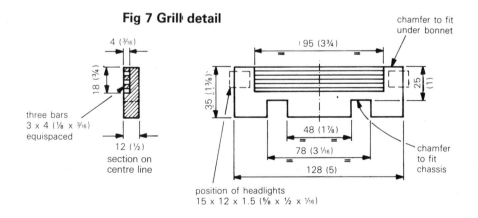

chamfer to fit under bonnet

4 (³⁄₁₆)

18 (¾)

three bars
3 x 4 (⅛ x ³⁄₁₆)
equispaced

12 (½)
section on
centre line

95 (3¾)

35 (1⅜)

25 (1)

48 (1⅞)

78 (3¹⁄₁₆)

128 (5)

chamfer
to fit
chassis

position of headlights
15 x 12 x 1.5 (⅝ x ½ x ¹⁄₁₆)

Fig 8 Body side
make one of each hand

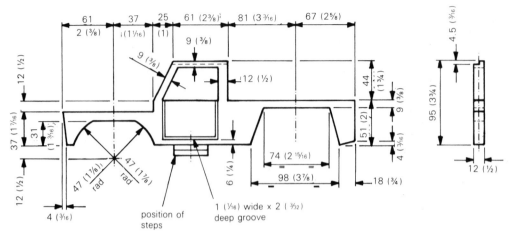

Fig 9 Front bumper

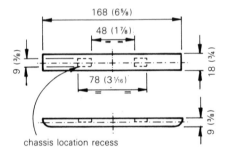

chassis location recess

Fig 10 Rear bumper
other dimensions as Fig 9

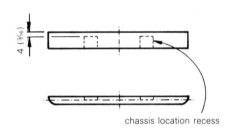

chassis location recess

longitudinal chassis members (Fig 4).

3 The tail gate (Fig 5) and the rear cab bulkhead (Fig 6) can now be cut out. Put these parts to one side until they are required for final assembly.

4 Make up the grill assembly (Fig 7). Use a chisel to remove the area where the three grill bars are to be fitted. Cut the grill bars slightly wider than required, glue them in position and sand them flush with the grill face when hardened.

The top face of each chassis locating slot (Fig 7) will have to be chamfered to enable it to fit tight against the top edge of the chassis. The correct amount of chamfering can only be arrived at by dry assembly onto the chassis in conjunction with the body side panels in Fig 8.

5 The headlights shown in Fig 7 can be cut out at this stage but they will not be

required until final assembly.

6 When you have cut out the body side panels, use a sharp trimming knife to cut the door outline.

7 Cut out the front and rear bumpers (Figs 9 and 10). Glue them to the assembled chassis.

8 Cut out and shape the bonnet (Fig 11).

9 Dry assemble onto chassis all previously cut out parts. (See Fig 4 for positions.) Use small clamps to temporarily secure the bonnet to the body sides while fitting the grill.

10 When you are satisfied with the dry assembly, glue previously cut parts together.

Stalwart Amphibious Truck (page 33), Off-road Racer (page 70), Trailer (page 85), Four-wheel-drive Vehicle (page 74)

Fig 11 Bonnet

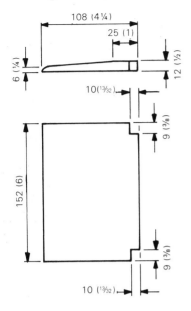

Fig 12 Floor layout
4 (³⁄₁₆) thick

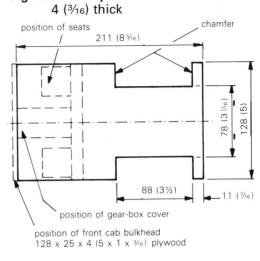

position of seats

chamfer

211 (8 ⁵⁄₁₆)

78 (3¹⁄₁₆)

128 (5)

88 (3½)

11 (⁷⁄₁₆)

position of gear-box cover

position of front cab bulkhead
128 x 25 x 4 (5 x 1 x ³⁄₁₆) plywood

Fig 13 Seat base
make two, 32 (1¼) wide

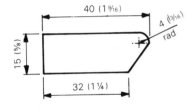

40 (1⁹⁄₁₆)

4 (³⁄₁₆) rad

15 (⁵⁄₈)

32 (1¼)

Fig 14 Seat backs
make two

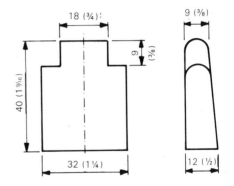

18 (¾)

9 (³⁄₈)

9 (³⁄₈)

40 (1⁹⁄₁₆)

32 (1¼)

12 (½)

Fig 15 Gear-box cover
63 (2⁷⁄₁₆) long

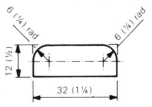

6 (¼) rad

6 (¼) rad

12 (½)

32 (1¼)

previous page Space Port Nasus 5 (page 59)

Pull-along Cart (page 106)

Fig 16 Console

Fig 17 Steering wheel assembly

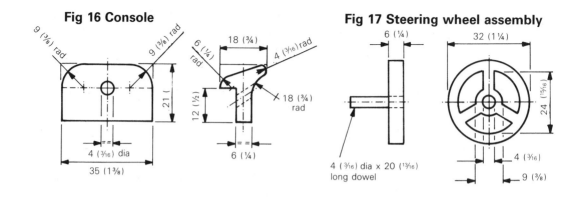

Fig 18 Assembled rear wheel arch

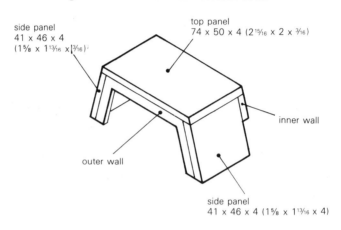

side panel
41 x 46 x 4
(1⅝ x 1¹³⁄₁₆ x ³⁄₁₆)

top panel
74 x 50 x 4 (2¹⁵⁄₁₆ x 2 x ³⁄₁₆)

inner wall

outer wall

side panel
41 x 46 x 4 (1⅝ x 1¹³⁄₁₆ x 4)

Fig 19 Rear wheel arch
(inner wall) make two, 4 (³⁄₁₆) thick

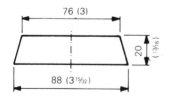

Fig 20 Rear wheel arch
(outer wall) make two, 4 (³⁄₁₆) thick

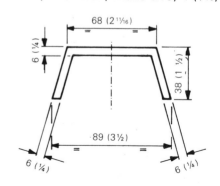

11 Cut out the front cab bulkhead and glue it in position underneath the bonnet overhang inside the cab.

12 Glue the floor in position (Fig 12). Do not chamfer the edges shown, until you are ready to fit the rear wheel arches.

13 Cut out, shape, and glue in position the two seats (Figs 13 and 14) and gear-box cover (Fig 15). (See Fig 12 for positioning of these parts.)

14 The console (Fig 16) is positioned on the bonnet edge in front of either seat, ie left- or right-hand drive. Glue the steering wheel assembly (Fig 17) into the console before final fitting.

15 The rear wheel arches (Figs 18, 19 and 20) must have all their parts cut out, chamfered, and dry assembled before final assembly of each complete wheel arch. Chamfer the floor as shown in Fig

12 to accept the wheel arch side panels.

16 Cut out, shape, and glue in position the front wheel arches (Fig 21).

17 Make, and glue in position the cab roof.

18 Cut out and make up the tow hitch assembly (Fig 23). Glue the assembly centrally underneath the rear of the vehicle.

19 Make the step assemblies (Fig 24), and glue them centrally underneath each cab door.

20 Cut to length the tail gate surround and rear body surrounds (see Cutting List). Glue them in position around the rear of the body (see colour photo page 77).

21 Glue the headlights in position (Fig 7). Cut out and glue the number plates (see Cutting List) centrally onto each bumper.

22 Smooth off all edges and varnish.

Fig 21 Front wheel arch
make two, 6 (¼) thick

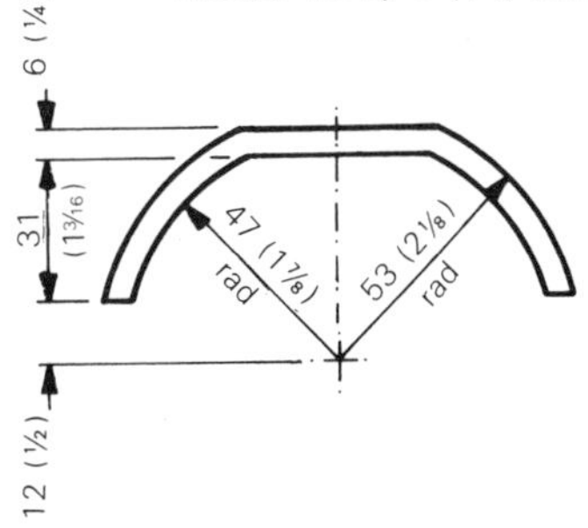

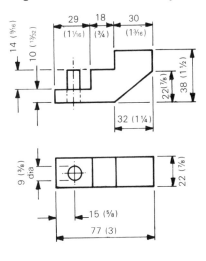

Fig 22 Cab roof

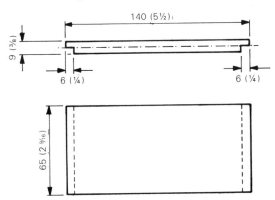

Fig 23 Tow hitch assembly

Fig 24 Cab step assembly
make two

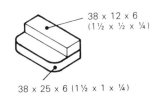

38 x 12 x 6
(1½ x ½ x ¼)

38 x 25 x 6 (1½ x 1 x ¼)

Cutting list

Longitudinal chassis member (Fig 1)	2 off	338×59×15mm (13⁵⁄₁₆×2³⁄₈×⁵⁄₈in)	Wood
Front cross member (Fig 2)	1 off	78×38×12mm (3¹⁄₁₆×1½×½in)	Wood
Rear cross member (Fig 3)	1 off	78×18×12mm (3¹⁄₁₆×¾×½in)	Wood
Tail gate (Fig 5)	1 off	128×45×12mm (5×1¾×½in)	Wood
Tail gate surround	1 off	162×4×4mm (6³⁄₈×³⁄₁₆×³⁄₁₆in)	Wood
Rear cab bulkhead (Fig 6)	1 off	128×68×12mm (5×2¹¹⁄₁₆×½in)	Wood
Front cab bulkhead	1 off	128×25×4mm (5×1×³⁄₁₆in)	Plywood
Grill (Fig 7)	1 off	128×35×12mm (5×1³⁄₈×½in)	Wood
	3 off	95×3×4mm (3¾×⅛×³⁄₁₆in)	Wood
Headlights	2 off	15×12×1.5mm (⁵⁄₈×½×¹⁄₁₆in)	Wood
Body side (Fig 8)	2 off	332×95×12mm (13×3¾×½in)	Wood
Rear body surround	2 off	154×4×4mm (4¹⁄₁₆×³⁄₁₆×³⁄₁₆in)	Wood
Bumpers (Figs 9–10)	2 off	168×18×9mm (6⁵⁄₈×¾×³⁄₈in)	Wood
Number plates	2 off	35×12×1.5mm (1³⁄₈×½×¹⁄₁₆in)	Wood
Bonnet (Fig 11)	1 off	108×152×12mm (4¼×6×½in)	Wood
Floor (Fig 12)	1 off	211×128×4mm (8⁵⁄₁₆×5×³⁄₁₆in)	Plywood
Seat base (Fig 13)	2 off	40×32×15mm (1⁹⁄₁₆×1¼×⁵⁄₈in)	Wood
Seat back (Fig 14)	2 off	40×32×12mm (1⁹⁄₁₆×1¼×½in)	Wood
Gear-box cover (Fig 15)	1 off	63×32×12mm (2⁷⁄₁₆×1¼×½in)	Wood
Console (Fig 16)	1 off	35×21×18mm (1³⁄₈×⅞×¾in)	Wood
Steering wheel (Fig 17)	1 off	32mm (1¼in) dia×6mm (¼in) thick	Wood
Steering column (Fig 17)	1 off	20mm (¹³⁄₁₆in) long×4mm (³⁄₁₆in) dia dowel	
Rear wheel arch (inner wall) (Fig 19)	2 off	88×20×4mm (3¹⁵⁄₁₆×¹³⁄₁₆×³⁄₁₆in)	Wood
side panel	2 off	41×46×4mm (1⁵⁄₈×1¹³⁄₁₆×³⁄₁₆in)	Wood
top panel	2 off	74×50×4mm (2¹⁵⁄₁₆×2×³⁄₁₆in)	Wood
outer wall (Fig 20)	2 off	89×38×4mm (3½×1½×³⁄₁₆in)	Wood
Front wheel arch (Fig 21)	2 off	106×37×6mm (4¼×1⁵⁄₁₆×¼in)	Wood
Cab roof (Fig 22)	1 off	140×65×9mm (5½×2⁹⁄₁₆×³⁄₈in)	Wood
Tow hitch (Fig 23)	1 off	77×38×22mm (3×1½×⅞in)	Wood
	1 off	25mm (1in) long×9mm (³⁄₈in) dia dowel	
Cab step (Fig 24)	2 off	38×12×6mm (1½×½×¼in)	Wood
	2 off	38×25×6mm (1½×1×¼in)	Wood

Ancillaries

Axles	2 off	158mm (6¼in) long×4mm (³⁄₁₆in) dia rod
Spring hub caps	4 off	suitable for 4mm (³⁄₁₆in) dia rod
Flat washers	16 off	inside diameter 4mm (³⁄₁₆in)
Wheels	4 off	76mm (3in) dia×35mm (1³⁄₈in) wide

TRAILER

This Trailer is designed to be towed by the Four-wheel-drive Vehicle (page 74) and carry the Off-road Racer (page 70). It can, however, carry other loads, extending its use and value as a play item.

As with the Four-wheel-drive Vehicle and Off-road Racer, matt varnish was used as a protective finish. When using screws on hardwood it is advisable to use pilot holes.

1 Cut the two side rails (Fig 1) to size and cut four recesses in each.
2 Cut the four chassis cross members (Fig 2) to size with a halving joint in the end of each one.
3 Assemble side rails and cross members.
4 Screw and glue axle blocks (Fig 3) in position underneath each side rail (see Fig 1). Glue 6mm (¼in) long×6mm (¼in) diameter dowel plugs into countersunk axle block retaining holes to cover screw heads.
5 Cut axles to length and insert them through both axle blocks.
6 Using the axles as a guide, place the wheel arch inner walls (Fig 4) over the axles and glue them in position.
7 Shape wheel arches (Fig 5). Glue them in position on top of the wheel arch inner walls.
8 Make two headboards (Fig 6). Using cup washers underneath your screw heads, screw and glue both headboards in place (see Fig 1).
9 Using the Cutting List as a guide, cut to size the three blocks that make up the tow-bar. Glue these blocks together as shown in Fig 7. Do not attempt to shape the tow-bar until the glue has hardened.
10 Glue the completed tow-bar centrally at one end of the Trailer (see Fig 2).
11 Smooth off all edges, and paint or varnish the Trailer before fitting wheels.
12 When fitting wheels, insert a flat washer between the wheel arch inner wall and the inside face of each wheel.

Fig 1 Part assembled side rail
make one of each hand

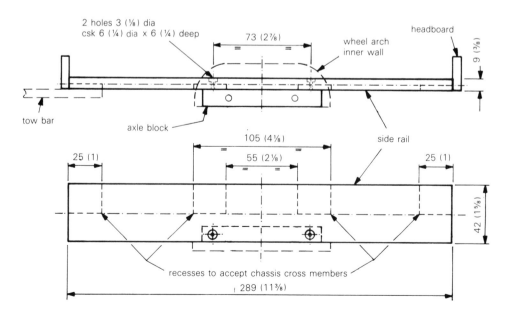

Fig 2 Chassis cross member
make four, 9 (⅜) thick

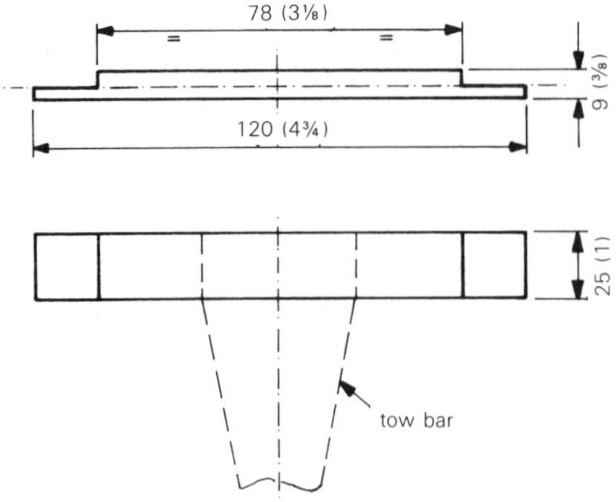

78 (3⅛)

120 (4¾)

9 (⅜)

25 (1)

tow bar

Fig 3 Axle block
make two, 12 (½) wide

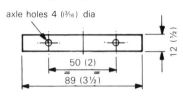

axle holes 4 (³⁄₁₆) dia

50 (2)

89 (3½)

12 (½)

Fig 4 Wheel arch inner wall
make two, 6 (¼) thick

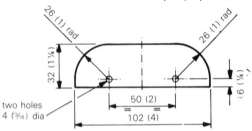

26 (1) rad

26 (1) rad

32 (1¼)

6 (¼)

two holes
4 (³⁄₁₆) dia

50 (2)

102 (4)

Fig 5 Wheel arch
make two, 23 (¹⁵⁄₁₆) wide

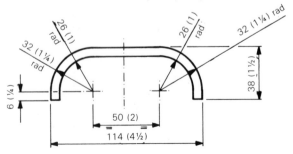

26 (1) rad

26 (1) rad

32 (1¼) rad

32 (1¼) rad

6 (¼)

38 (1½)

50 (2)

114 (4½)

Fig 6 Headboard
make two, 6 (¼) thick

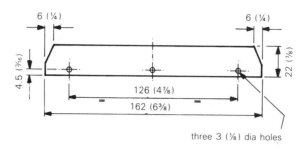

three 3 (⅛) dia holes

Fig 7 Assembled tow-bar

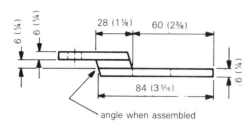

angle when assembled

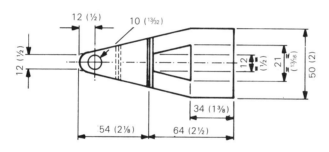

Cutting list

Side rail (Fig 1)	2 off	289×42×9mm (11⅜×1⅝×⅜in)	Wood
Cross members (Fig 2)	4 off	120×25×9mm (4¾×1×⅜in)	Wood
Axle block (Fig 3)	2 off	89×12×12mm (3½×½×½in)	Wood
Plugs	4 off	6mm (¼in) long×6mm (¼in) dia dowel	
Wheel arch inner wall (Fig 4)	2 off	102×32×6mm (4×1¼×¼in)	Wood
Wheel arch (Fig 5)	2 off	114×38×23mm (4½×1½×¹⁵⁄₁₆in)	Wood
Headboard (Fig 6)	2 off	162×21×6mm (6⅜×⅞×¼in)	Wood
Tow-bar (Fig 7)	1 off	84×50×6mm (3⁵⁄₁₆×2×¼in)	Wood
	1 off	28×50×6mm (1⅛×2×¼in)	Wood
	1 off	54×50×6mm (2⅛×2×¼in)	Wood

Ancillaries

Axles	2 off	208mm (8³⁄₁₆)×4mm (³⁄₁₆in) dia metal rod
Spring hub caps	4 off	suitable for 4mm (³⁄₁₆in) dia rod
Wheels	4 off	model aeroplane type 45mm (1¾in) dia
Cup washers	6 off	suitable for No 4 size screws
Flat washers	4 off	inside diameter 4mm (³⁄₁₆in)

TRAFFIC LIGHTS GAME

Traffic Lights is a game I have derived from the knock 'em down principle of coconut shys that are to be found at most local fairs and fêtes. All of the family can enjoy playing this game, and because the assembly can be taken apart, you won't have to leave it behind if you go out for the day in your car.

The game has been an instant success with my children and their friends. They were playing with it before it was painted, and I had to bribe them so that I could take it away for painting!

The permutations of Traffic Lights are many. Lights can either be knocked down in order, red, yellow, green, etc, or all of one colour can be knocked down, or horizontal rows, or vertical rows. Numbers can also be added to each traffic light for scoring.

Another variation of play when all the lights have been knocked flat is to try and put them all back up again using the balls. Soft sponge balls should be used because other types are too heavy. Soft sponge ones also allow you to play the game indoors when the weather is inclement.

Skill, various techniques and coordination can all be learned as play progresses.

1 Cut to size the two side panels (Fig 1) and cut out the 6mm (¼in) wide slots. Slots must be tight enough to hold the cross panels firmly in position, but not too tight that the game can not easily be taken apart manually.

2 Cut out and make up three cross panel assemblies (Figs 2–3).

3 Screw one magnetic catch to each of the nine catch mounting blocks (Fig 4). (See Fig 7.)

4 Glue and screw three catch mounting blocks (Fig 4) to each cross panel (Fig 2) in the centre of each 51mm (2in) hinge recess (Fig 7).

5 Make eighteen corner blocks (Fig 5), and glue one each side of each catch mounting block (Fig 7).

6 Cut out the nine traffic lights, and glue a hinge pad to each (Fig 6).

7 Screw flush fitting hinges to the traffic lights (Fig 7), then screw each completed traffic light to the hinge mounting battens (Fig 7).

8 Most magnetic catch plates are flat on one face and have two raised points on the other face; these points are to mark the correct position of the plate to enable it to locate onto the magnetic catch accurately.

To find the fixing position of a catch plate, place the plate onto the magnetic

Fig 1 Side panels
make two, 6 (¼) thick

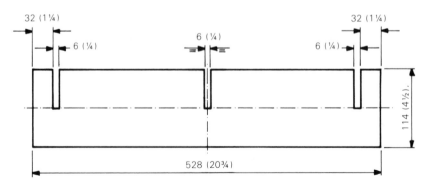

32 (1¼)   6 (¼)   32 (1¼)

6 (¼)   6 (¼)

114 (4½)

528 (20¾)

Fig 2 Cross panels
make three, 6 (¼) thick

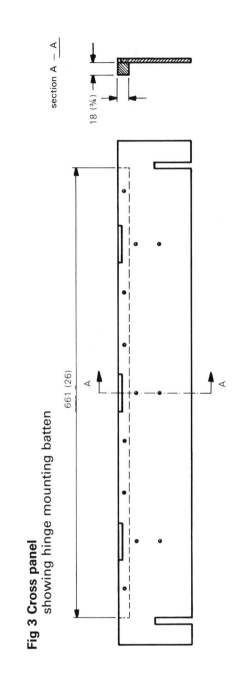

twelve 4 (³/₁₆) dia csk holes

571 (22½)
292 (11½)
140 (5½)
51 (2)
51 (2)
51 (2)
51 (2)
433 (17)
737 (29)
86 (3⅜)
6 (¼)
6 (¼)
6 (¼)
32 (1¼)
32 (1¼)
9 (⅜)
114 (4½)

section A — A
18 (¾)

Fig 3 Cross panel
showing hinge mounting batten

661 (26)
A
A

Fig 4 Catch mounting block
make nine, 8 (¾) thick

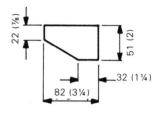

83 (3¼)
25 (1)
18 (¾)
57 (2¼)
57 (2¼)
83 (3¼)

Fig 5 Corner block
make eighteen, 18 (¾) thick

22 (⅞)
51 (2)
32 (1¼)
82 (3¼)

Fig 6 Traffic lights
make nine

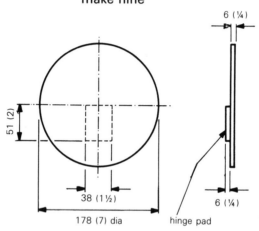

51 (2)
6 (¼)
38 (1½)
6 (¼)
178 (7) dia
hinge pad

Fig 7 Assembled traffic light

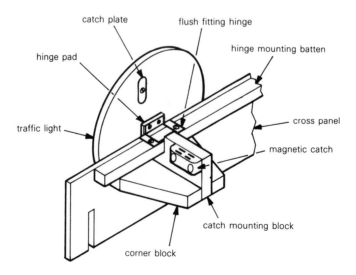

catch plate
flush fitting hinge
hinge pad
hinge mounting batten
traffic light
cross panel
magnetic catch
catch mounting block
corner block

catch with the raised points facing upwards. Close the traffic-light disc onto the catch plate and press hard. Remove the catch plate from the magnetic catch and place it on top of the marks made in the traffic-light disc. This will be the correct fixing position and the catch plate can now be screwed in position.

9 The easiest way of painting this project is with it assembled. Discs should be placed flat against their magnetic catches.

Cutting list

Side panels (Fig 1)	2 off	528×114×6mm (20¾×4½×¼in)	Plywood
Cross panels (Fig 2)	3 off	737×114×6mm (29×4½×¼in)	Plywood
Hinge mounting battens (Fig 3)	3 off	661×18×18mm (26×¾×¾in)	Wood
Catch mounting blocks (Fig 4)	9 off	83×83×18mm (3¼×3¼×¾in)	Wood
Corner blocks (Fig 5)	18 off	82×51×18mm (3¼×2×¾in)	Wood
Traffic lights (Fig 6)	9 off	178mm (7in) dia×6mm (¼in) thick	Plywood
Hinge pads (Fig 6)	9 off	38×51×6mm (1½×2×¼in)	Plywood

Ancillaries

Magnetic catches (Fig 7)	9 off
Flush fitting hinges (Fig 7)	9 off

DOLLS' BUNK BEDS

Children learn about life by mimicking most things that happen to them through play, including bed time. Although often not very keen to go to bed themselves, children tend to have very firm ideas on when and where their toys should sleep.

This bunk-bed project will give dolly a good night's sleep, and also provide a desk top for her to do her homework, or use as a dressing table. A wardrobe with hanging rail and clothes hangers has been included underneath the bed so that all of dolly's clothes can be hung up and kept clean and tidy.

1 Cut out bed base (Fig 2). Screw and glue battens in position as shown, using a piece of 6mm (¼in) plywood as a spacer when fixing the battens that will form the wardrobe panel location slots (see Fig 3).

Screws do not have to be in any precise position, but care must be taken when fitting battens that screw positions do not conflict when assembling.

2 Cut out back panel (Fig 3). Screw and glue battens in position as in step 1.

3 Make up side panel (Fig 4).

4 Cut out and assemble side panel (left) (Fig 5), and wardrobe side panel (left)

Fig 1 View of assembled bunk

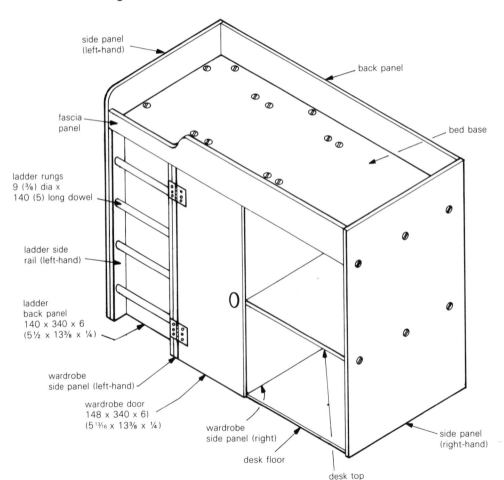

side panel (left-hand)

back panel

fascia panel

bed base

ladder rungs 9 (⅜) dia x 140 (5) long dowel

ladder side rail (left-hand)

ladder back panel 140 x 340 x 6 (5½ x 13⅜ x ¼)

wardrobe side panel (left-hand)

wardrobe door 148 x 340 x 6 (5¹³⁄₁₆ x 13⅜ x ¼)

wardrobe side panel (right)

desk floor

side panel (right-hand)

desk top

Fig 2 Bed base assembly
6 (¼) thick

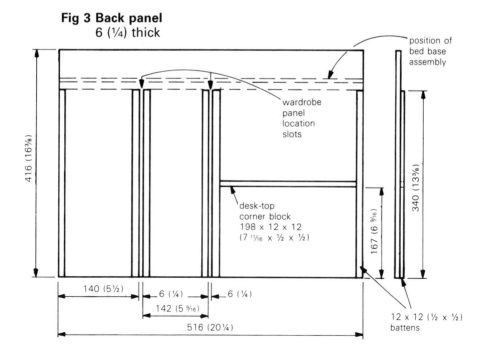

142 (5 %6)

140 (5½)   6 (¼)   6 (¼)

base

12 x 12 (½ x ½)
battens

516 (20¼)

242 (9½)

Fig 3 Back panel
6 (¼) thick

position of
bed base
assembly

416 (16⅜)

wardrobe
panel
location
slots

340 (13⅜)

desk-top
corner block
198 x 12 x 12
(7 ¹¹⁄₁₆ x ½ x ½)

167 (6 %6)

140 (5½)   6 (¼)   6 (¼)

142 (5 %6)

516 (20¼)

12 x 12 (½ x ½)
battens

Fig 4 Side panel (right-hand)
6 (¼) thick

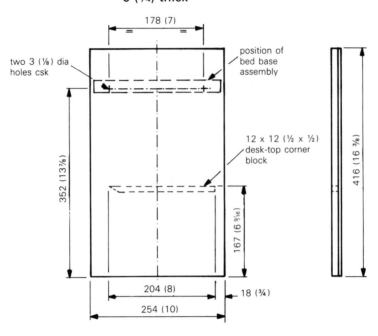

178 (7)

two 3 (⅛) dia
holes csk

position of
bed base
assembly

12 x 12 (½ x ½)
desk-top corner
block

352 (13⅞)

416 (16 ⅜)

167 (6 ⁹⁄₁₆)

204 (8)

18 (¾)

254 (10)

Fig 5 Side panel (left-hand)
6 (¼) thick

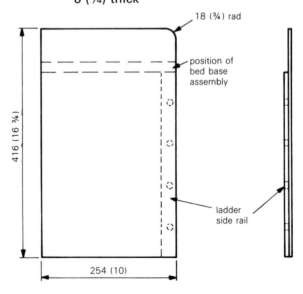

18 (¾) rad

position of
bed base
assembly

416 (16 ¾)

ladder
side rail

254 (10)

Fig 6 Ladder side rail
(right-hand) make one of each hand
6 (¼) thick, hardwood

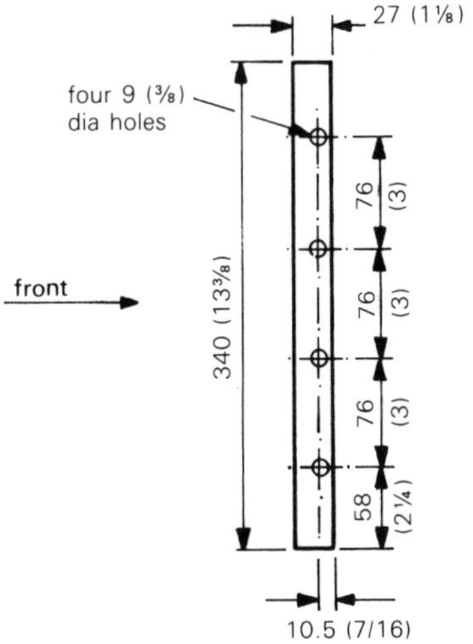

27 (1⅛)

four 9 (⅜)
dia holes

front

76 (3)

76 (3)

76 (3)

58 (2¼)

340 (13⅜)

10.5 (7/16)

Fig 7 Wardrobe side panel
(left-hand) 6 (¼) thick

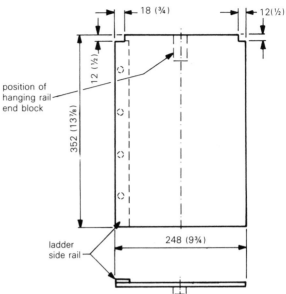

18 (¾)

12(½)

12 (½)

position of
hanging rail
end block

352 (13⅞)

ladder
side rail

248 (9¾)

Fig 8 Wardrobe side panel
(right-hand) 6 (¼) thick

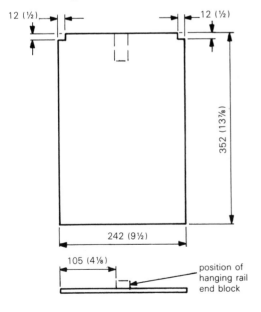

12 (½)

12 (½)

352 (13⅞)

242 (9½)

105 (4⅛)

position of
hanging rail
end block

Fig 9 Desk floor
6 (¼) thick

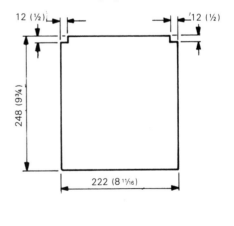

12 (½)

12 (½)

248 (9¾)

222 (8 11/16)

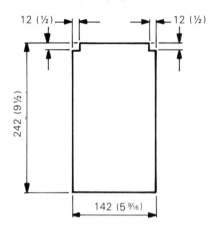

Fig 10 Wardrobe floor
6 (¼) thick

12 (½) ➞ | ← | → | ← 12 (½)

242 (9½)

142 (5 9⁄16)

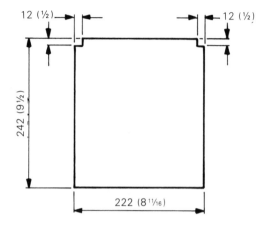

Fig 11 Desk top
6 (¼) thick

12 (½) ➞ | ← | → | ← 12 (½)

242 (9½)

222 (8 11⁄16)

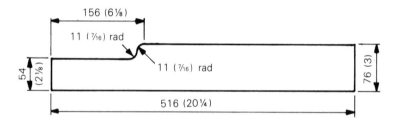

Fig 12 Fascia panel
6 (¼) thick

156 (6⅛)

11 (7⁄16) rad

11 (7⁄16) rad

54 (2⅛)

76 (3)

516 (20¼)

(Fig 7). When making these panels it is preferable to use hardwood for the ladder side rails (Fig 6).

5 Screw and glue assembled back panel (Fig 3), bed base (Fig 2), side panel (right) (Fig 4) and wardrobe side panel (left) (Fig 7) together. (See Fig 1 for assembled view.)

6 Cut ladder rungs to length (Fig 1).

7 Insert ladder rungs into ladder side rail (right) (Fig 6), and screw and glue side panel (left) (Fig 5) to previously assembled parts.

8 Cut to size ladder back panel (Fig 1) and glue in place.

9 Cut to size wardrobe side panel (Fig 8), wardrobe floor (Fig 10), and glue them both in position.

10 Cut to size desk floor (Fig 9) and desk top (Fig 11), and glue them in position.

11 When glueing fascia panel (Fig 12) in position, do not use screws. Hold panel in position with small clamps until glue has hardened.

12 Screw hinges to wardrobe door, making sure that any screw protruding on the inside is filed down.

13 Place wardrobe door in position and insert remaining hinge screws.

14 Make the hanging rail end blocks, and cut hanging rail to length. Glue in position inside the wardrobe (Figs 7 and 8).

15 Mark and cut out as many clothes hangers as you require, making sure that each one is a loose fit on the hanging rail. Children do not have a lot of patience, therefore a tight-fitting hanger could end in disaster.

Fig 13 Hanging rail end block

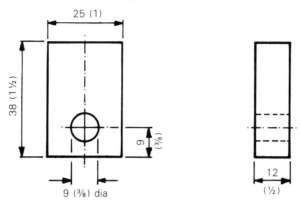

25 (1)

38 (1½)

9 (³⁄₈)

9 (³⁄₈) dia

12 (½)

Hanging rail 142 (5⁹⁄₁₆) long x 9 (³⁄₈) dia dowel

Fig 14 Clothes hanger
4 (³⁄₁₆) thick

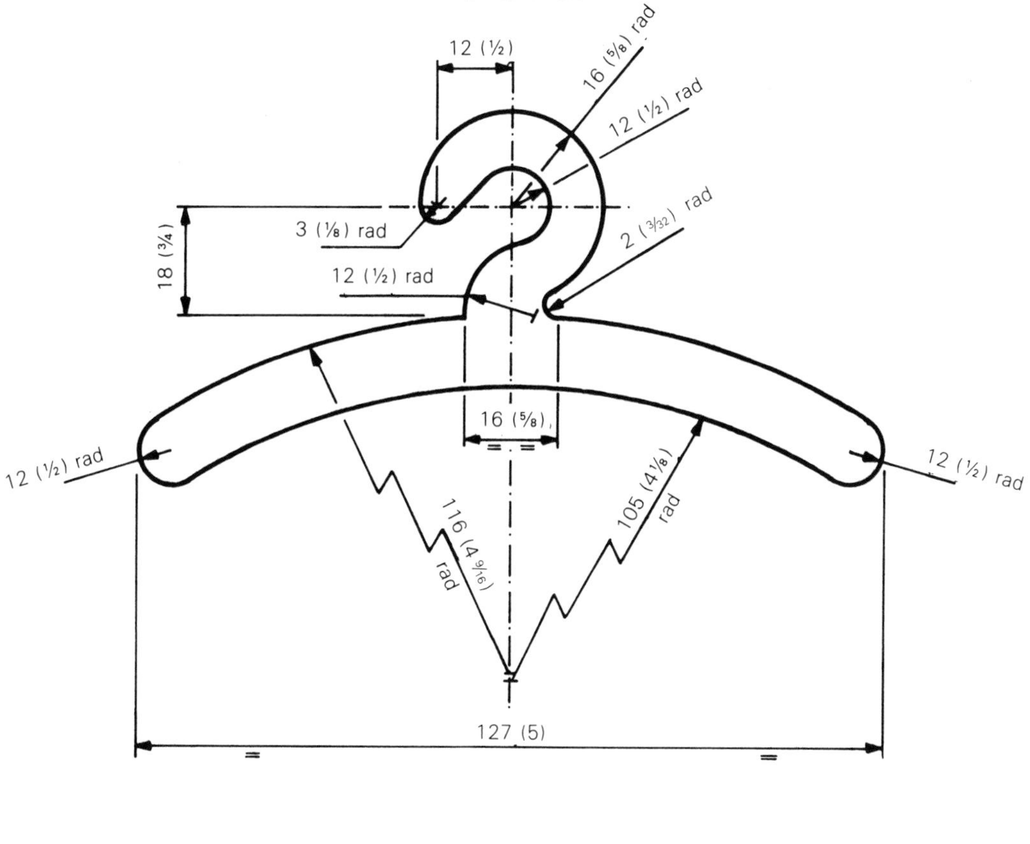

12 (½)

16 (⁵⁄₈) rad

12 (½) rad

3 (⅛) rad

2 (³⁄₃₂) rad

12 (½) rad

18 (¾)

16 (⁵⁄₈)

12 (½) rad

116 (4 ⁹⁄₁₆) rad

105 (4⅛) rad

12 (½) rad

127 (5)

Cutting list

Bed base (Fig 2)	1 off	516×242×6mm (20¼×9½×¼in)	Plywood
battens (Fig 2)	2 off	516×12×12mm (20¼×½×½in)	Wood
battens (Fig 2)	6 off	218×12×12mm (8½×½×½in)	Wood
Back panel (Fig 3)	1 off	516×416×6mm (20¼×16⅜×¼in)	Plywood
battens (Fig 3)	6 off	340×12×12mm (13⅜×½×½in)	Wood
desk-top corner block (Fig 3)	1 off	198×12×12mm (7¹¹⁄₁₆×½×½in)	Wood
Side panel (right-hand) (Fig 4)	1 off	254×416×6mm (10×16⅜×¼in)	Plywood
desk-top corner block (Fig 4)	1 off	204×12×12mm (8×½×½in)	Wood
Side panel (left-hand) (Fig 5)	1 off	254×416×6mm (10×16⅜×¼in)	Plywood
Ladder side rail (Fig 6)	2 off	27×340×6mm (1⅛×13⅜×¼in)	Hardwood
Wardrobe side panel (left-hand) (Fig 7)	1 off	248×352×6mm (9¾×13⅞×¼in)	Plywood
Wardrobe side panel (right-hand) (Fig 8)	1 off	242×352×6mm (9½×13⅞×¼in)	Plywood
Desk floor (Fig 9)	1 off	222×248×6mm (8¹¹⁄₁₆×9¾×¼in)	Plywood
Wardrobe floor (Fig 10)	1 off	142×242×6mm (5⁹⁄₁₆×9½×¼in)	Plywood
Desk top (Fig 11)	1 off	222×242×6mm (8¹¹⁄₁₆×9½×¼in)	Plywood
Fascia panel (Fig 12)	1 off	516×76×6mm (20¼×3×¼in)	Plywood
Hanging rail end block (Fig 13)	2 off	25×38×12mm (1×1½×½in)	Wood
Clothes hangers (Fig 14)		make from 127×62×4mm (5×2⁷⁄₁₆×³⁄₁₆in)	Plywood

Ancillaries

Hinges (Fig 1)	2 off	38mm (1½in) long	

TABLE

Designed to be used with the Chair project (page 102), this table gives children real wooden furniture of their own. Time and time again my children's table has proved a very useful addition around the house. It is small and light, and can easily be moved to any part of the house for immediate use. When it is not being monopolised by the children, this table can be used as an attractive occasional table for everyday use.

Storage isn't a problem with this table because the legs are detachable, so when your children are too old to use it anymore, it can easily be dismantled and stored away for their children.

1 Start by cutting to size the table top (Fig 1).
2 Drill and countersink the sixteen 3mm (⅛in) dia holes in the table top (Fig 1). Sand smooth before final assembly.
3 Cut to size and shape sides A (Fig 2), and sides B (Fig 3). Do not drill the 9mm (⅜in) dia dowel holes until the table is assembled.
4 Using four temporary corner blocks (see Cutting List), glue and screw together the four sides in their relevant positions as shown in Fig 1.
5 Screw and glue table top in position.
6 Drill 9mm (⅜in) dia dowel holes 38mm (1½in) deep as shown in Figs 2–3. Cut dowels to length and glue them into the dowel holes.
7 Cut the legs to length and round off their corners.
8 Remove the temporary corner blocks, and screw the legs into the corners. Do not glue legs in position. Use cup washers underneath the leg-retaining screws as these give the finished table a more professional appearance.
9 Smooth off all edges, then paint or varnish.

Cutting list

Base (Fig 1)	1 off	482×482×6mm (19×19×¼in)	Plywood
Sides A (Fig 2)	2 off	506×102×25mm (20×4×1in)	Wood
Sides B (Fig 3)	2 off	506×102×25mm (20×4×1in)	Wood
Temporary corner blocks	4 off	84×42×42mm (3¼×1⅝×1⅝in)	Wood
Dowel pegs	12 off	38mm (1½in) long×9mm (⅜in) dia dowel	
Legs	4 off	458×42×42mm (18×1⅝×1⅝in)	Wood

Fig 1 Top
6 (¼) thick

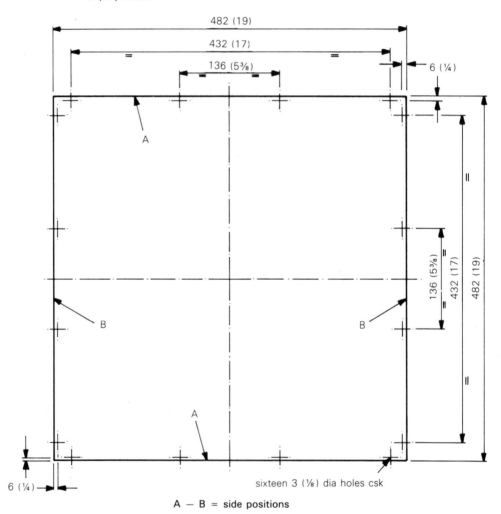

482 (19)

432 (17)

136 (5⅜)

6 (¼)

A

136 (5⅜)

432 (17)

482 (19)

B

B

A

6 (¼)

sixteen 3 (⅛) dia holes csk

A — B = side positions

legs
make four, 458 (18) x 42 (1⅝) x 42 (1⅝)

100

Fig 2 Side A
make two

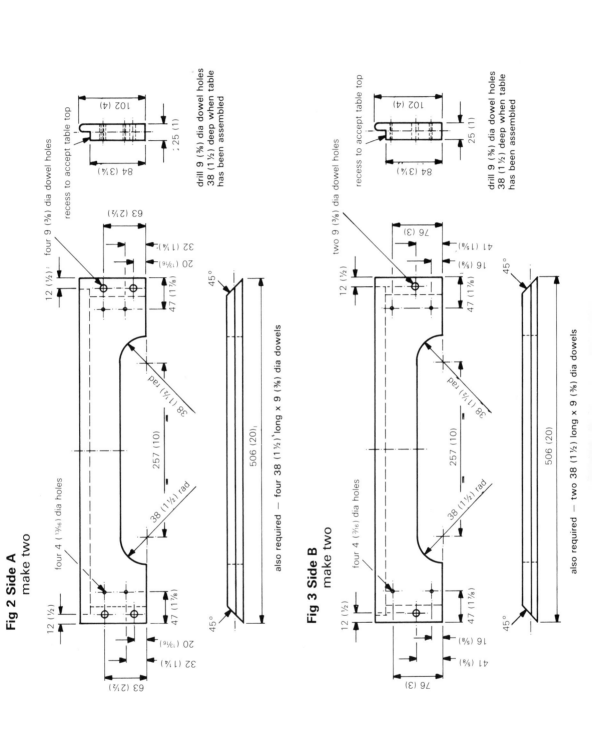

recess to accept table top

drill 9 (⅜) dia dowel holes
38 (1½) deep when table
has been assembled

102 (4)

25 (1)

84 (3¼)

63 (2½)

four 9 (⅜) dia dowel holes

12 (½)

32 (1¼)

20 (¹³⁄₁₆)

47 (1⅞)

45°

38 (1½) rad

257 (10)

38 (1½) rad

506 (20)

four 4 (³⁄₁₆) dia holes

12 (½)

47 (1⅞)

20 (¹³⁄₁₆)

32 (1¼)

63 (2½)

45°

also required — four 38 (1½) long × 9 (⅜) dia dowels

Fig 3 Side B
make two

recess to accept table top

drill 9 (⅜) dia dowel holes
38 (1½) deep when table
has been assembled

102 (4)

25 (1)

84 (3¼)

76 (3)

two 9 (⅜) dia dowel holes

12 (½)

41 (1⅝)

16 (⅝)

47 (1⅞)

45°

38 (1½) rad

257 (10)

38 (1½) rad

506 (20)

four 4 (³⁄₁₆) dia holes

12 (½)

47 (1⅞)

16 (⅝)

41 (⅝)

76 (3)

45°

also required — two 38 (1½) long × 9 (⅜) dia dowels

CHAIR and BENCH

Initially the Chair and Bench for this project were designed and made for a local playgroup, but my children enjoyed using them so much that I had to build other chairs and a bench for them too. Although they are very simple in their construction, both the Chair and Bench are very strong and, especially when used

with the Table (page 99), will give years of pleasure.

Children like having their own personal belongings and there is plenty of scope to personalise each child's chair. All holes on the drawings are shown countersunk, but cup washers can be used if preferred (see colour photo page 130).

Fig 1 Assembled chair/bench sides 12 (½) thick
make one of each hand per chair/bench

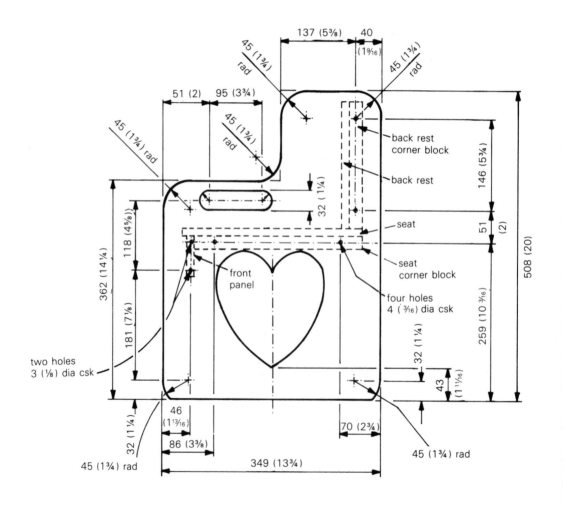

Fig 2 Heart

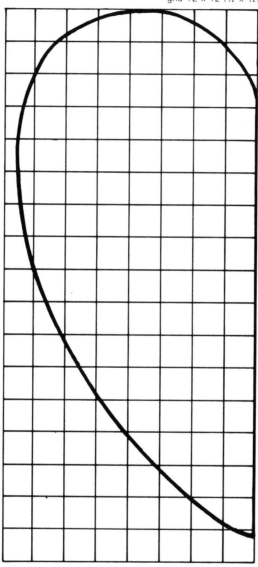

Cutting list

Sides (chair and bench)
(Fig 1)	2 off	508×349×12mm (20×13¾×½in)	Plywood
Chair seat (Fig 3)	1 off	360×290×12mm (15⅛×11½×½in)	Plywood
corner blocks	2 off	272×18×18mm (10¾×¾×¾in)	Wood
Chair back rest (Fig 4)	1 off	410×210×12mm (16⅛×8¼×½in)	Plywood
corner blocks	2 off	210×18×18mm (8¼×¾×¾in)	Wood
	2 off	410×18×18mm (16⅛×¾×¾in)	Wood
Chair front panel	1 off	410×70×12mm (16⅛×2¾×½in)	Plywood
Bench seat (Fig 5)	1 off	800×290×12mm (31½×11½×½in)	Plywood
corner blocks	2 off	272×18×18mm (10¾×¾×¾in)	Wood
Bench back rest (Fig 6)	1 off	800×218×12mm (31½×8¼×½in)	Plywood
corner blocks	2 off	210×18×18mm (8¼×¾×¾in)	Wood
	1 off	800×18×18mm (31½×¾×¾in)	Wood
Bench front panel	1 off	800×70×12mm (31½×2¾×½in)	Plywood

103

Fig 3 Chair seat
12 (½) thick

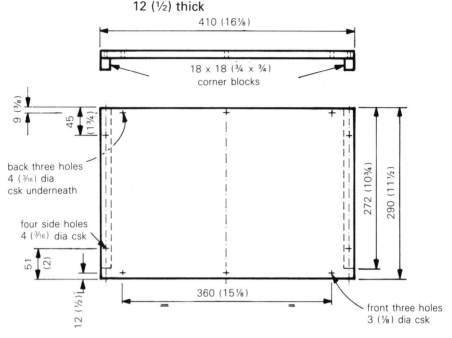

18 x 18 (¾ x ¾)
corner blocks

back three holes
4 (³⁄₁₆) dia
csk underneath

four side holes
4 (³⁄₁₆) dia csk

front three holes
3 (⅛) dia csk

Fig 4 Chair back rest
12 (½) thick

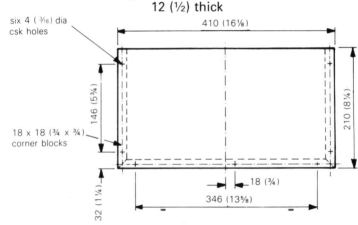

six 4 (³⁄₁₆) dia
csk holes

18 x 18 (¾ x ¾)
corner blocks

Chair front panel 410 x 70 x 12 (16⅛ x 2¾ x ½)

1 The side panels (Fig 1) are the same dimensions for both the chair and bench. Mark and cut out two side panels for each chair or bench you make.

2 To mark the heart shape (Fig 2) on each side panel, draw a full-size grid onto a piece of card and transpose the heart one square at a time. Cut out the heart and use it as a template.

3 When making up the seats (Figs 3 or 5), countersink the three holes along the back edge from underneath.

4 All corner blocks shown should be made from hardwood which will make the chairs stronger and more durable. Drill pilot holes in all hardwood corner blocks in their respective positions.

5 Cut out and assemble a back rest (Figs 4 and 6) and a chair or bench front panel (see Cutting List).

6 Assemble your bench or chair, smooth off all edges and varnish.

Fig 5 Bench seat 12 (½) thick

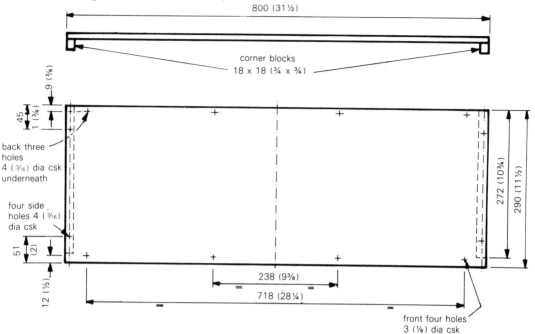

800 (31½)

corner blocks
18 x 18 (¾ x ¾)

9 (⅜)

45
1 (¾)

272 (10¾)
290 (11½)

back three
holes
4 (³⁄₁₆) dia csk
underneath

four side
holes 4 (³⁄₁₆)
dia csk

51
(2)

12 (½)

238 (9⅜)

718 (28¼)

front four holes
3 (⅛) dia csk

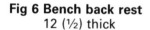

bench front panel 800 x 70 x 12 (31½ x 2¾ x ½)

Fig 6 Bench back rest
12 (½) thick

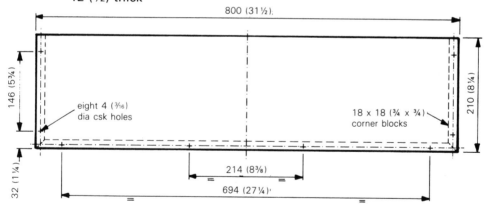

800 (31½)

146 (5¾)

210 (8¼)

eight 4 (³⁄₁₆)
dia csk holes

18 x 18 (¾ x ¾)
corner blocks

32 (1¼)

214 (8⅜)

694 (27¼)

PULL-ALONG CART

This cart is designed for children to transport their toys etc. Children must not be allowed to ride on it themselves.

On completion of this project it was immediately put into service and load tested by by children. Loading things into and onto vehicles, etc and then moving their loads from one place to another is a favourite pastime with my children. In their imagination they are delivery persons, delivering supplies to various imaginary friends.

Helping Daddy is not a regular practice of my children, but when they were using their Pull-along Cart they were quite willing to help me clean out my workshop, albeit for only about half an hour!

1 Start by cutting the base to size (Fig 1). Drill all of the holes shown in both Fig 1 and Fig 2, countersinking where required.

2 Make two short sides and two long sides (Fig 3). Shaping of the top edges is best done when the cart is assembled.
3 Make the corner plates (Fig 15).
4 Screw and glue the sides to the base. The corner plates can be screwed in position at this stage while the sides are being glued. Use round head screws for final fitting of corner plates
5 Cut out and shape the rear cross member (Fig 4) and the rear axle supports (Fig 5). Slot, screw and glue them together.
6 The completed rear cross member assembly is now screwed and glued to the base (Fig 2).
7 Cut to size both steering plates (Fig 6). Screw and glue one of them to the base (Fig 2).
8 Screw and glue the front axle bearers (Fig 8) to the front axle beam (Fig 7).
9 As shown in Figs 12–14, screw and glue

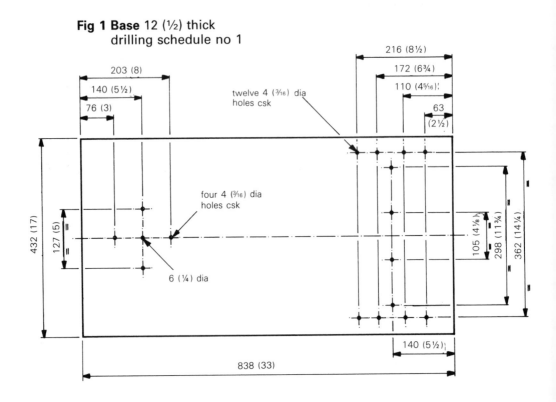

Fig 1 Base 12 (½) thick
drilling schedule no 1

216 (8½)

203 (8)

172 (6¾)

140 (5½)

110 (4⁵⁄₁₆)!

76 (3)

twelve 4 (³⁄₁₆) dia holes csk

63 (2½)

four 4 (³⁄₁₆) dia holes csk

432 (17)

127 (5)

105 (4⅛)

298 (11¾)

362 (14¼)

6 (¼) dia

140 (5½)!

838 (33)

Fig 2 Base
drilling schedule no 2

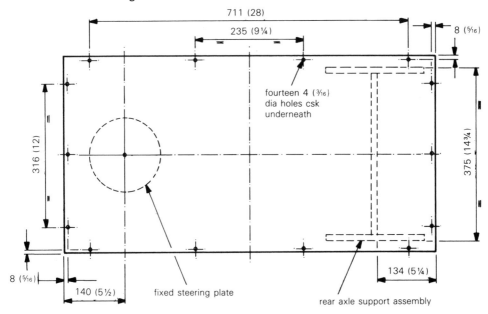

711 (28)

235 (9¼)

8 (⁵⁄₁₆)

fourteen 4 (³⁄₁₆)
dia holes csk
underneath

316 (12)

375 (14¾)

8 (⁵⁄₁₆)

140 (5½)

fixed steering plate

134 (5¼)

rear axle support assembly

Fig 3 Sides
make two of each length

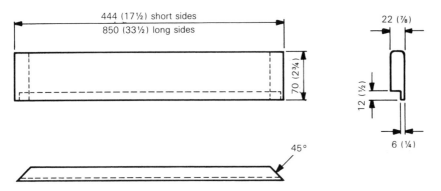

444 (17½) short sides

850 (33½) long sides

70 (2¾)

22 (⅞)

12 (½)

6 (¼)

45°

Fig 4 Rear cross member
12 (½) thick

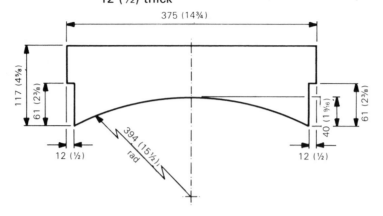

Fig 5 Rear axle support
make two, 12 (½) thick

Fig 6 Steering plate
make two, 12 (½) thick

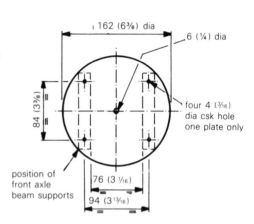

the steering-bar supports (Fig 9) to the front axle beam supports (Fig 10).

10 Screw and glue each front axle beam support assembly to the moving steering plate (Fig 6). (See also Figs 12–14.)

11 The assembled front axle beam (Fig 7) can now be screwed and glued in position. (See Figs 12–14.)

12 Bolt the completed steering assembly to the fixed steering plate using the steering bolt and a nylon insert nut. This type of nut will not work loose during use. (Nylon insert nuts are also known as 'Simmonds patent nuts' after the person who invented them, or 'Nylock nuts' which is a trade name.)

13 The steering bar handle is inserted into the steering bar 12mm (½in) dia hole. Secure the handle using a small countersunk screw inserted from underneath the steering bar.

14 Join the steering bar to the steering-bar supports using the steering-bar pin (Fig 14). Fit flat washers between the steering bar and the steering-bar supports (Fig 14).

15 Remove the corner plates when you are ready to varnish/paint, and replace them when the varnishing/painting has been completed.

16 When fitting the wheels it is necessary to put a flat washer between the cart and the inside face of each wheel hub.

Fig 7 Front axle beam

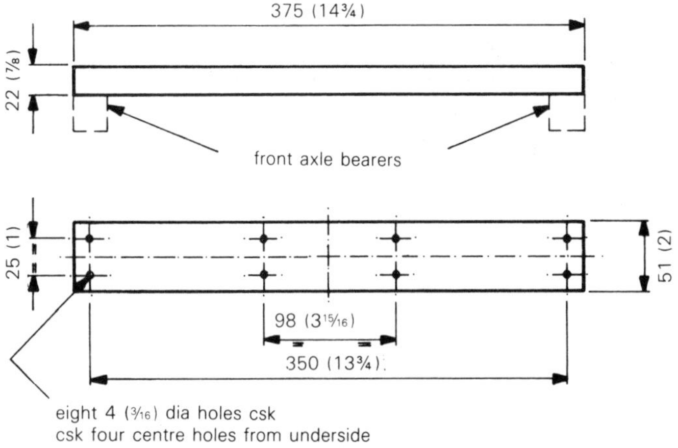

375 (14¾)

22 (⅞)

front axle bearers

25 (1)

51 (2)

98 (3¹⁵⁄₁₆)

350 (13¾)

eight 4 (³⁄₁₆) dia holes csk
csk four centre holes from underside

Fig 8 Front axle bearer
make two

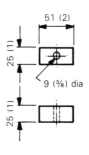

51 (2)

25 (1)

9 (⅜) dia

25 (1)

Fig 9 Steering-bar supports
make two

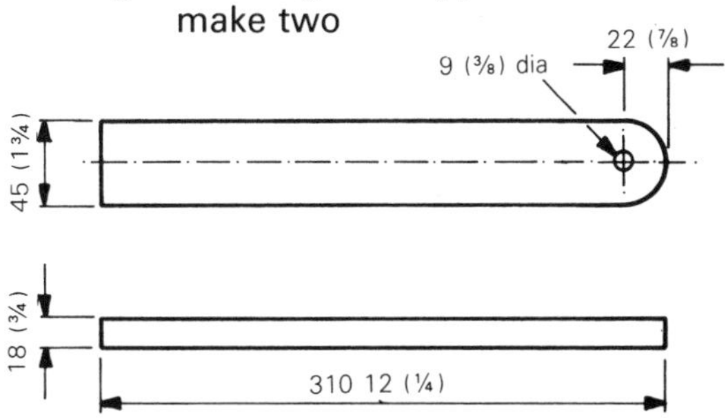

22 (⅞)

9 (⅜) dia

45 (1¾)

18 (¾)

310 12 (¼)

Fig 10 Front axle beam support
make two, 18 (¾) thick

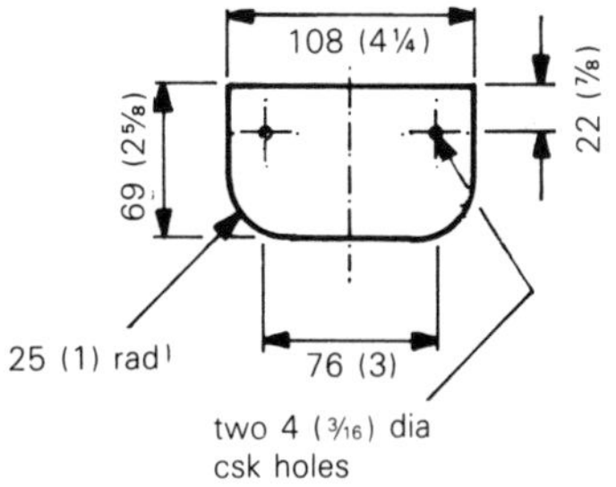

108 (4¼)

22 (⅞)

69 (2⅝)

25 (1) rad¹

76 (3)

two 4 (³⁄₁₆) dia
csk holes

Fig 11 Steering bar

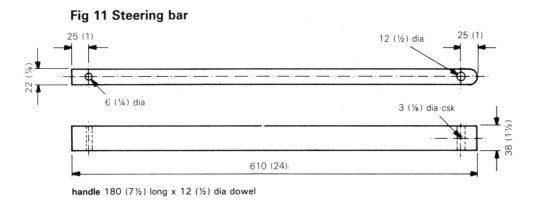

25 (1)

12 (½) dia

25 (1)

22 (⅞)

6 (¼) dia

3 (⅛) dia csk

38 (1½)

610 (24)

handle 180 (7½) long x 12 (½) dia dowel

109

Fig 12 Assembled front axle and steering detail
front view

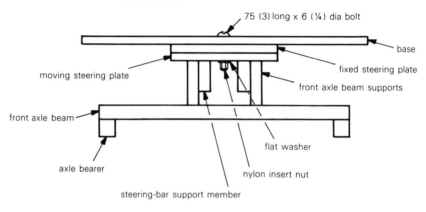

75 (3) long x 6 (¼) dia bolt

base

moving steering plate

fixed steering plate

front axle beam supports

front axle beam

flat washer

axle bearer

nylon insert nut

steering-bar support member

Fig 13 Assembled front axle and steering detail
side view

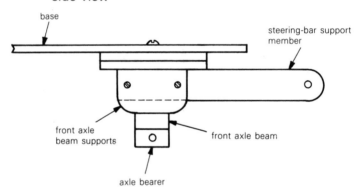

base

steering-bar support member

front axle beam supports

front axle beam

axle bearer

Fig 14 Assembled front axle and steering detail
base, pivot and fixed steering plate removed

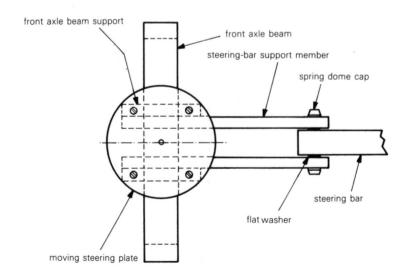

front axle beam support

front axle beam

steering-bar support member

spring dome cap

steering bar

flat washer

moving steering plate

Fig 15 Corner plates
make four (aluminium)

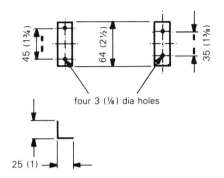

four 3 (⅛) dia holes

25 (1)

Cutting list

Base (Figs 1–2)	1 off	838×432×12mm (33×17×½in)	Plywood
Short sides (Fig 3)	2 off	444×70×22mm (17½×2¾×⅞in)	Wood
Long sides (Fig 3)	2 off	850×70×22mm (33½×2¾×⅞in)	Wood
Rear cross member (Fig 4)	1 off	375×117×12mm (14¾×4⅝×½in)	Plywood
Rear axle supports (Fig 5)	2 off	222×152×12mm (8¾×6×½in)	Plywood
Steering plates (Fig 6)	2 off	162mm (6⅜in) dia×12mm (½in) thick	Plywood
Front axle beam (Fig 7)	1 off	375×51×22mm (14¾×2×⅞in)	Wood
Front axle bearers (Fig 8)	2 off	51×25×25mm (2×1×1in)	Wood
Steering-bar supports (Fig 9)	2 off	310×45×18mm (12¼×1¾×¾in)	Wood
Front axle beam supports (Fig 10)	2 off	108×69×18mm (4¼×2⅝×¾in)	Wood
Steering bar (Fig 11)	1 off	610×38×22mm (24×1½×⅞in)	Wood
Steering-bar handle	1 off	180mm (7½in) long×12mm (½in) dia dowel	

Ancillaries

Axles	2 off	391mm (15⅜in) long×9mm (⅜in) dia steel rod
Spring dome caps	6 off	to suit 9mm (⅜in) dia rod
Flat washers	6 off	9mm (⅜in) inside diameter
	1 off	6mm (¼in) inside diameter
Steering bolt (Fig 12)	1 off	(roofing bolt type) 75mm (3in) long×6mm (¼in) dia
Nylon insert nut (Fig 12)	1 off	to suit 6mm (¼in) dia steering bolt
Steering-bar pin	1 off	91mm (3⁹⁄₁₆in) long×9mm (⅜in) dia steel rod
Wheels	4 off	159mm (6¼in) dia
Corner plates (Fig 15)	4 off	45×25×25mm (1¾×1×1in) angle aluminium

SPIRIT OF AMERICA WRECKER TRUCK

The Spirit of America is a custom wrecker truck built on an Autocar DC7384 chassis equipped with tandem front and rear axles. This chassis arrangement meant that greater gross vehicle weights could be achieved over conventional three-axle vehicles. Only 115 of these chassis were ever built by Autocar and the Spirit of America is one of only two wrecker configurations using this chassis.

Detailed plans of the prototype vehicle and its chassis were impossible to obtain because the DC7384 chassis was originally built in 1964, and is now no longer in production. For this reason some of the finer detail of the original vehicle may be missing on this model as it was built from photographs and a limited amount of information supplied by Volvo GM Heavy Truck Corporation USA. If more structural information regarding this vehicle is available to you, I am sure that your model would benefit from its inclusion.

Although the emphasis of this book is on toy projects made from wood, the use of some metal parts is inevitable when building a model of this calibre, and unavoidable where strength and minimum thickness of material are required. Stainless steel should be used in preference to mild steel because of its bright appearance and resistance to corrosion. Refer to Methods and Materials (page 8) for hints on working with metal. When fitting spring dome caps, slightly rounding off shaft ends etc will be helpful.

To achieve a first-class, durable model, use only hardwood for construction, and seal with three coats of matt varnish for protection.

1 Test (dry) assembly is most important in the construction of this model. Do not therefore glue, or pin, any part in position until it has been test assembled.

2 Mark both sides of each joint as it is made A–A, B–B etc. This simple procedure is essential when making joints and it will ensure correct final assembly.

3 Begin by making the chassis longitudinal members (Fig 1). For accuracy when marking positions of cut outs and recesses, clamp longitudinal chassis members side by side.

4 Make the first and third cross members (Fig 4), but do not glue them in position at this stage. Screw the front wheel pivot plates (Fig 5) in position as shown (Fig 6) using round head self tapping screws.

5 Cut out and glue in position (see Fig 2) the second cross member (Fig 7), the fourth and fifth cross members (Fig 9) and the rear body panel (Fig 10).

6 Insert the rear bogie pivot rod into the chassis and using the rod as a guide, glue both rear bogie spacer blocks in position.

7 Screw and glue the rear crash bar supports (Fig 12) into the rear body panel (Fig 10) as shown in Fig 2. Cut to length the rear crash bar (Fig 13) and drill pilot holes to accept the screwed eyes. Screw the crash bar in position, centrally between the rear crash bar supports, then screw the screwed eyes into the pilot holes.

8 Make two rear wheel bogies (Fig 14).

9 Insert the rear bogie pivot rod through the chassis and rear bogie spacer blocks. Place the rear wheel bogies onto the pivot pin, and secure them in position using spring dome caps. Leave sufficient gap between each spacer and bogies to ensure free movement of the bogies.

10 Make two front axle beams (Fig 15). Place them in position as shown in Fig 6. Insert front axle pivot pins into assembly and test its operation. Do not fit spring dome caps at this stage.

11 Before making the front axle block assemblies (Figs 17–19), it is necessary to increase the depth of the slots in the steering plate retaining screws. This is because the screw heads must be filed flush with the steering plates when in position, and removal of the plates may be necessary at a future date.

12 Fit a spring dome cap to one end of each stub axle. Then insert the stub axles into the axle blocks (Fig 16). Place a flat spacer washer over each exposed shaft before fitting the wheels, and spring dome caps.

Fig 1 Chassis longitudinal member
make one of each hand, 16 (⁵/₈) thick

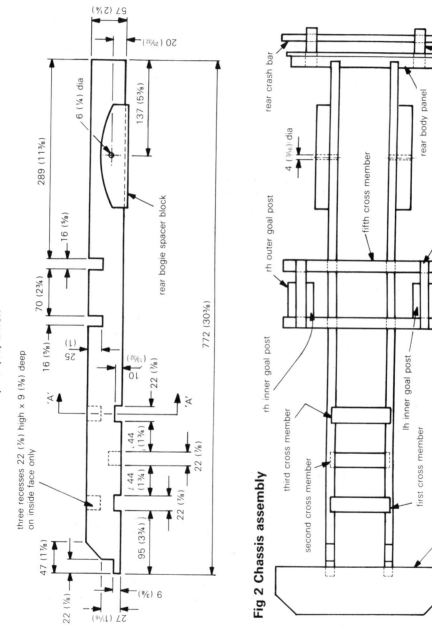

three recesses 22 (⁷/₈) high × 9 (³/₈) deep on inside face only

47 (1⁷/₈)

22 (⁷/₈)

27 (1¹/₁₆)

9 (³/₈)

95 (3¾)

22 (⁷/₈)

22 (⁷/₈)

44 (1¾)

44 (1¾)

10

13/₃₂

25 (1)

16 (⁵/₈)

'A'

'A'

70 (2¾)

16 (⁵/₈)

289 (11³/₈)

137 (5³/₈)

6 (¼) dia

rear bogie spacer block

20 (²⁵/₃₂)

57 (2¼)

772 (30³/₈)

Fig 2 Chassis assembly

rear crash bar

rear crash-bar supports

rear body panel

4 (³/₁₆) dia

fifth cross member

goal-post support member

rh outer goal post

lh outer goal post

rh inner goal post

lh inner goal post

third cross member

second cross member

fourth cross member

first cross member

front bumper

Fig 3 Section A-A
showing assembly position
for first and third cross members

Fig 4 First and third cross members
make one of each, 22 (⅞) thick

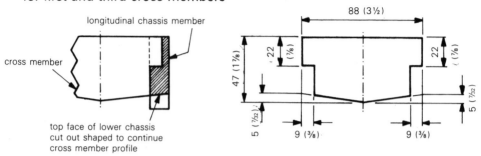

longitudinal chassis member

cross member

top face of lower chassis
cut out shaped to continue
cross member profile

88 (3½)

47 (1⅞)

22 (⅞)

22 (⅞)

5 (⁷⁄₃₂)

5 (⁷⁄₃₂)

9 (⅜)

9 (⅜)

Fig 5 Front wheel pivot plates
1.5 (¹⁄₁₆) thick stainless steel
make two pairs

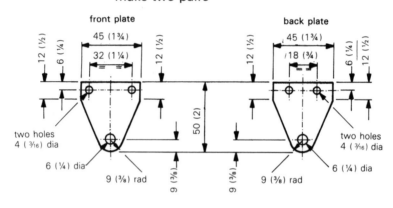

front plate

back plate

12 (½)

6 (¼)

45 (1¾)

32 (1¼)

12 (½)

12 (½)

45 (1¾)

18 (¾)

6 (¼)

12 (½)

two holes
4 (³⁄₁₆) dia

6 (¼) dia

50 (2)

two holes
4 (³⁄₁₆) dia

6 (¼) dia

9 (⅜) rad

9 (⅜)

9 (⅜)

9 (⅜) rad

Fig 6 First and third cross members
showing positions of wheel pivot plates

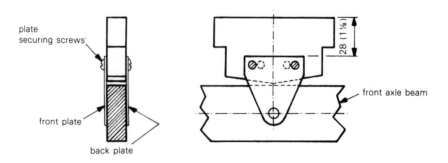

plate
securing screws

front plate

back plate

front axle beam

28 (1⅛)

Fig 7 Second cross member

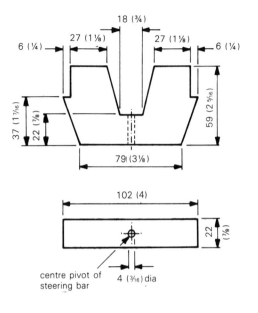

centre pivot of steering bar

4 (³⁄₁₆) dia

Fig 8 Goal-post support member
make two, 12 (½) thick

lh outer face shown

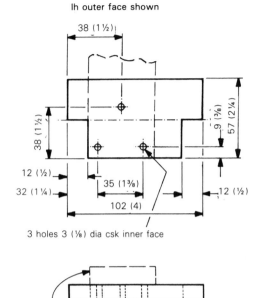

3 holes 3 (⅛) dia csk inner face

position of goal posts

Fig 9 Fourth and fifth cross members
make one of each, 16 (⅝) thick

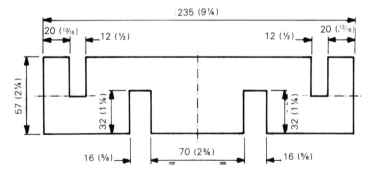

Fig 10 Rear body panel

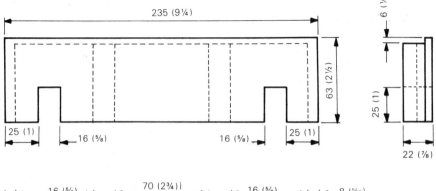

235 (9¼)

63 (2½)

25 (1)

25 (1)

16 (⅝)

16 (⅝)

25 (1)

6 (¼)

25 (1)

22 (⅞)

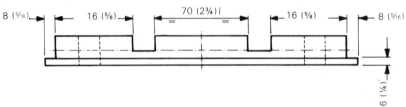

8 (⁵⁄₁₆)

16 (⅝)

70 (2¾)

16 (⅝)

8 (⁵⁄₁₆)

6 (¼)

Fig 11 Rear bogie spacer block
make two, 25 (1) thick

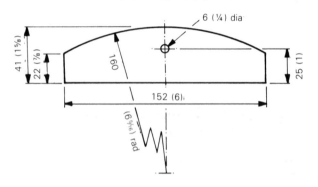

6 (¼) dia

41 (1⅝)

22 (⅞)

160

25 (1)

152 (6)

(6⁵⁄₁₆) rad

Fig 12 Rear crash-bar supports
make two

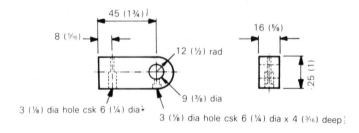

45 (1¾)

8 (⁵⁄₁₆)

12 (½) rad

16 (⅝)

25 (1)

9 (⅜) dia

3 (⅛) dia hole csk 6 (¼) dia

3 (⅛) dia hole csk 6 (¼) dia x 4 (³⁄₁₆) deep

116

Fig 13 Rear crash-bar assembly

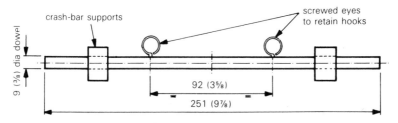

crash-bar supports

screwed eyes
to retain hooks

9 (⅜) dia dowel

92 (3⅝)

251 (9⅞)

Fig 14 Rear-wheel bogie
make two, 16 (⅝) thick

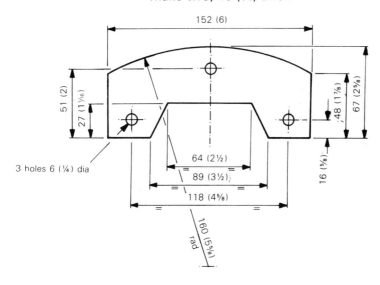

152 (6)

51 (2)

27 (1¹⁄₁₆)

48 (1⅞)

67 (2⅝)

16 (⅝)

3 holes 6 (¼) dia

64 (2½)

89 (3½)

118 (4⅝)

160 (5⅝) rad

Fig 15 Front axle beam
make two

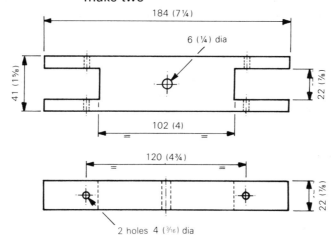

184 (7¼)

6 (¼) dia

41 (1⅝)

22 (⅞)

102 (4)

120 (4¾)

22 (⅞)

2 holes 4 (³⁄₁₆) dia

117

Fig 16 Tandem steering assembly

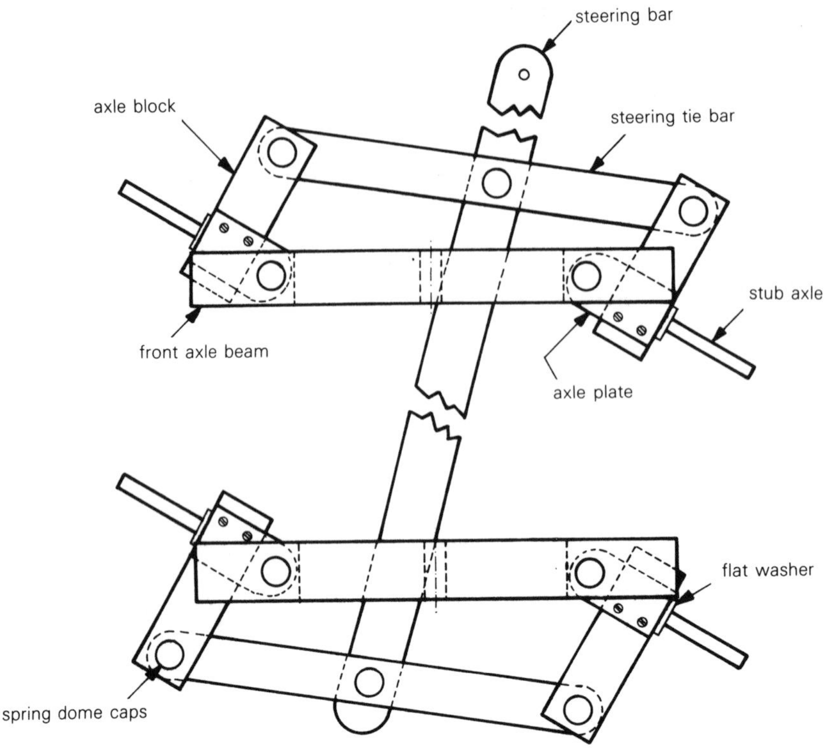

steering bar
axle block
steering tie bar
stub axle
front axle beam
axle plate
flat washer
spring dome caps

Fig 17 Front axle block
showing steering plate positions
make two of each hand

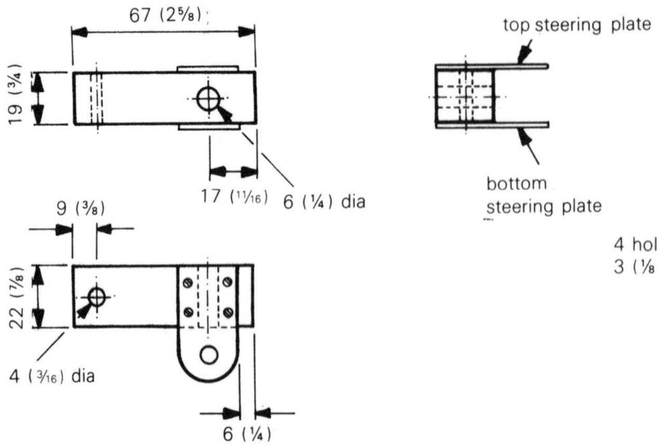

67 (2⅝)
19 (¾)
17 (11/16)
6 (¼) dia
9 (⅜)
22 (⅞)
4 (3/16) dia
6 (¼)
top steering plate
bottom steering plate

Fig 18 Top steering plate
1.5 (1/16) thick stainless steel
make four

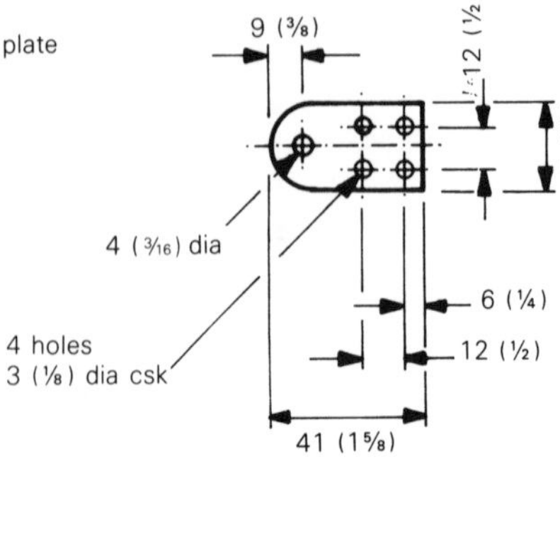

9 (⅜)
12 (½)
22 (⅞)
4 (3/16) dia
4 holes
3 (⅛) dia csk
6 (¼)
12 (½)
41 (1⅝)

Fig 19 Bottom steering plate
1.5 (1/16) thick
stainless steel, make four

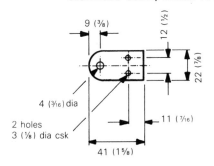

9 (3/8)

12 (1/2)

22 (7/8)

4 (3/16) dia

2 holes
3 (1/8) dia csk

11 (7/16)

41 (1 5/8)

Fig 20 Steering tie bar
make two, 12 (1/2) thick

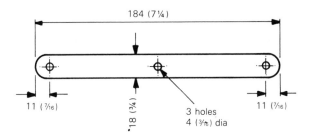

184 (7 1/4)

11 (7/16)

18 (3/4)

3 holes
4 (3/16) dia

11 (7/16)

Fig 21 Steering bar
12 (1/2) thick

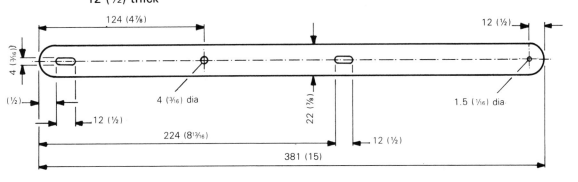

124 (4 7/8)

12 (1/2)

4 (3/16)

(1/2)

4 (3/16) dia

22 (7/8)

1.5 (1/16) dia

12 (1/2)

224 (8 13/16)

12 (1/2)

381 (15)

119

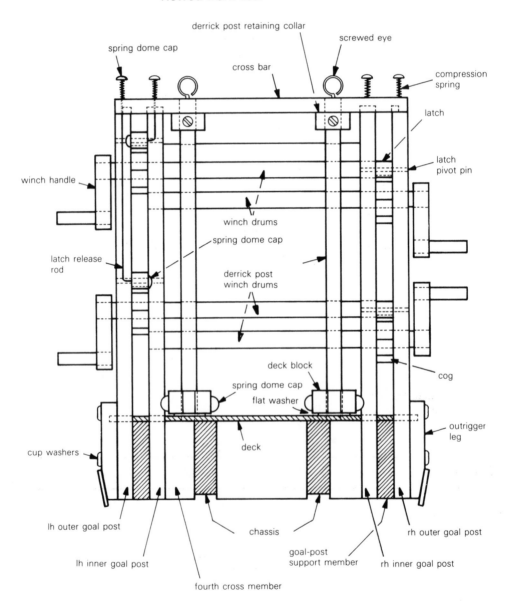

Fig 22 Assembled goal posts
viewed from rear

derrick post retaining collar

screwed eye

spring dome cap

cross bar

compression spring

latch

latch pivot pin

winch handle

winch drums

spring dome cap

latch release rod

derrick post winch drums

deck block

cog

spring dome cap

flat washer

cup washers

outrigger leg

deck

lh outer goal post

chassis

rh outer goal post

lh inner goal post

goal-post support member

rh inner goal post

fourth cross member

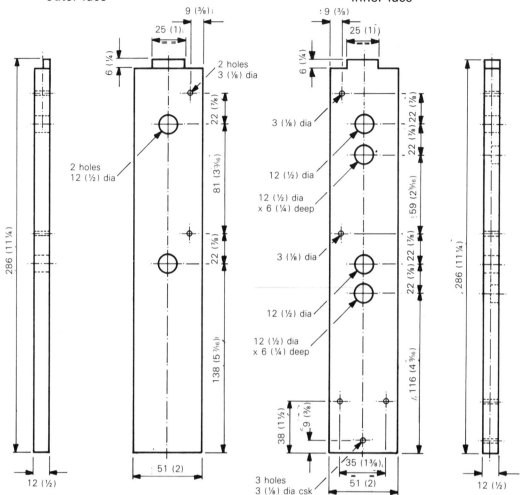

Fig 23 Left-hand outer goal post
outer face

Fig 24 Left-hand inner goal post
inner face

Fig 23 labels:
9 (3/8)
25 (1)
6 (1/4)
2 holes 3 (1/8) dia
22 (7/8)
2 holes 12 (1/2) dia
81 (3 3/16)
22 (7/8)
286 (11 1/4)
138 (5 7/16)
51 (2)
12 (1/2)

Fig 24 labels:
9 (3/8)
25 (1)
6 (1/4)
3 (1/8) dia
22 (7/8)
22 (7/8)
12 (1/2) dia
12 (1/2) dia x 6 (1/4) deep
59 (2 5/16)
3 (1/8) dia
22 (7/8)
22 (7/8)
12 (1/2) dia
12 (1/2) dia x 6 (1/4) deep
116 (4 9/16)
286 (11 1/4)
38 (1 1/2)
9 (3/8)
35 (1 3/8)
51 (2)
3 holes 3 (1/8) dia csk
12 (1/2)

13 Final fit each complete axle block assembly into the front axle beams (Fig 16), using the front axle block pivot pins.
14 Final fit the first, and third cross members into the chassis assembly (Fig 2).
15 Final fit assembled front axle beams to the first and third cross members (Figs 6 and 16), using the front axle beam pivot pins. Fit one spring dome cap to each front axle pivot pin before assembling. Use a clamp to fit the remaining spring dome caps onto the pivot pins.
16 Cut to length and fit in position the steering tie bars, using the front axle block to steering tie bar connecting pins (Fig 16).
17 Connect the steering bar to the steering tie bars and second cross member (Fig 16). (See Cutting List for sizes of connecting pins.) If steering movement is stiff, liberally coat moving surfaces with teak oil.
18 Insert rear axles into rear wheel bogies. Fit wheels and spring dome caps. Again, teak oil can be used to ease axle movement.
19 Make the goal posts (Figs 23–6). It is

121

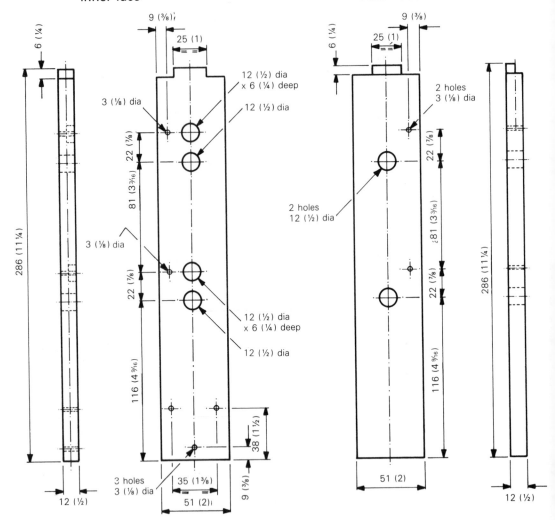

Fig 25 Right-hand inner goal post
inner face

Fig 26 Right-hand outer goal post
outer face

important to label the face of each goal post as it is being made to avoid confusion when assembling.

20 To assemble goal posts, screw and glue the outside goal posts to the outer face of each goal-post support member (Fig 8). Screw through the inside face of the goal-post support member, ensuring that screw heads are flush. Now screw and glue the inner goal posts in position using the winch drums to ensure correct alignment of goal-post holes.

21 Mark, cut out and place in position, the deck (Fig 27). Do not final fit at this stage.

22 Make the deck headboard (Fig 28). Do not final fit at this stage.

23 Cut out the rear body side panels (Fig 30), and the front body side panels (Fig 31). Test fit, then final assemble with the deck (Fig 27). Squeeze the screwed eyes around the grab rails to retain them in position.

24 Screw the ladders (Fig 32) in position (Fig 31) using 9mm (⅜in) round head screws. When making the ladders, drill as many holes as possible in the areas to be removed.

25 Screw and glue the jacking legs (Fig

Fig 27 Deck showing headboard position
6 (¼) thick

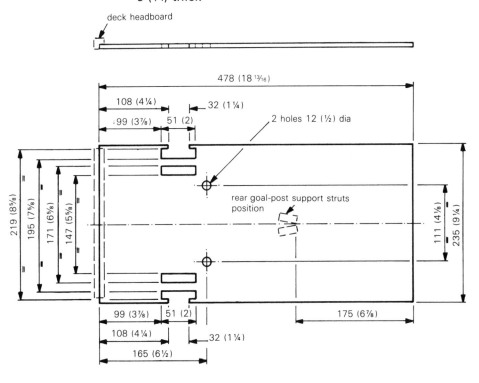

Fig 28 Deck headboard

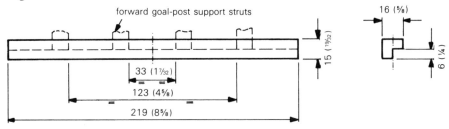

Fig 29 Side view of assembled deck headboard
showing forward strut position

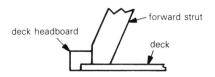

Fig 30 Rear body side panel
make one of each hand

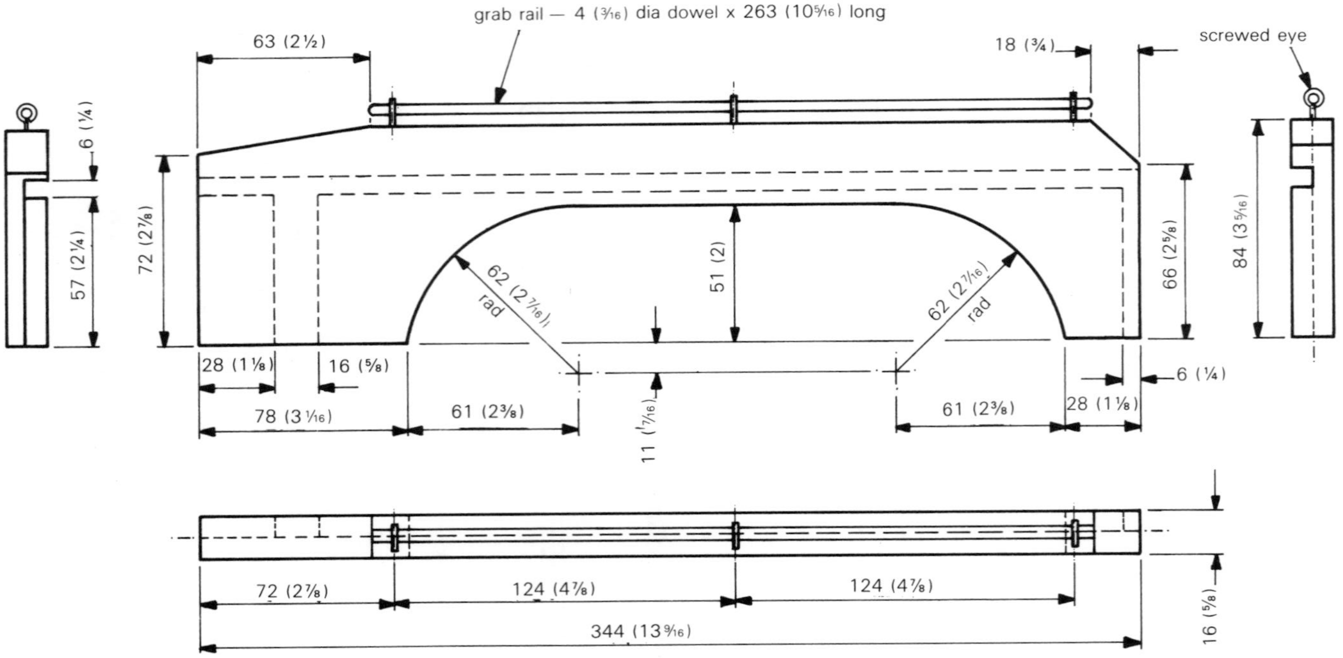

screwed eye

84 (3⁵⁄₁₆)

66 (2⁵⁄₈)

6 (¹⁄₄)

28 (1¹⁄₈)

61 (2³⁄₈)

62 (2⁷⁄₁₆) rad

18 (³⁄₄)

grab rail — 4 (³⁄₁₆) dia dowel × 263 (10⁵⁄₁₆) long

51 (2)

11 (⁷⁄₁₆)

62 (2⁷⁄₁₆) rad

61 (2³⁄₈)

16 (⁵⁄₈)

78 (3¹⁄₁₆)

28 (1¹⁄₈)

63 (2½)

72 (2⁷⁄₈)

6 (¹⁄₄)

57 (2¼)

16 (⁵⁄₈)

124 (4⁷⁄₈)

124 (4⁷⁄₈)

344 (13⁹⁄₁₆)

72 (2⁷⁄₈)

Fig 31 Front body side panels
make one of each hand

grab rail
4 (³⁄₁₆) dowel x 116 (4 ⁹⁄₁₆) long lhs
4 (³⁄₁₆) dia dowel x 97 (3 ¹³⁄₁₆) long rhs

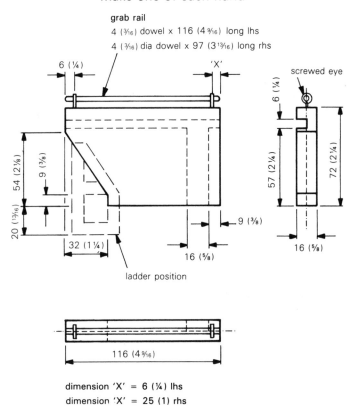

ladder position

dimension 'X' = 6 (¼) lhs
dimension 'X' = 25 (1) rhs

Fig 32 Ladder
make two, 1.5 (¹⁄₁₆) thick stainless steel

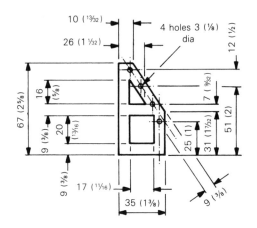

Fig 33 Assembled jacking leg
make two

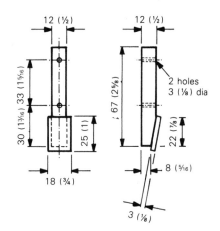

125

Fig 34 Cog
make four, 11 (⁷⁄₁₆) thick

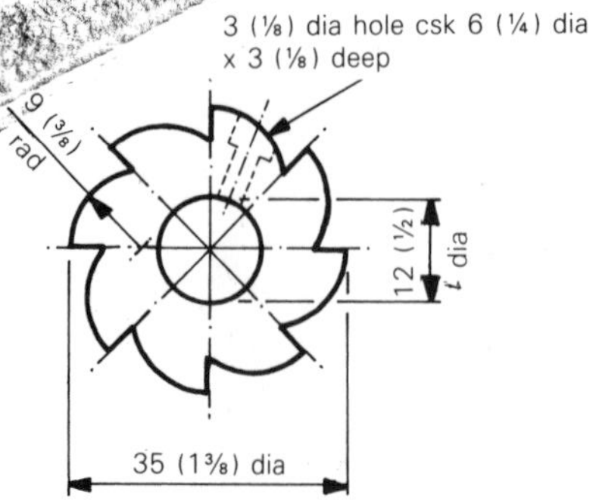

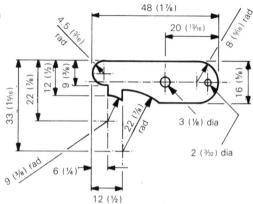

3 (⅛) dia hole csk 6 (¼) dia
x 3 (⅛) deep

9 (³⁄₈) rad

12 (½)

t dia

35 (1⅜) dia

Fig 35 Latch
make four, 11 (⁷⁄₁₆) thick

48 (1⅞)

4.5 (³⁄₁₆) rad

20 (¹³⁄₁₆)

8 (⁵⁄₁₆) rad

33 (1⁵⁄₁₆)

22 (⅞)

12 (½)

9 (⅜)

16 (⅝)

22 (⅞) rad

3 (⅛) dia

2 (³⁄₃₂) dia

9 (⅜) rad

6 (¼)

12 (½)

latch pivot pins see cutting list

Fig 36 Winch handle assembly
make four

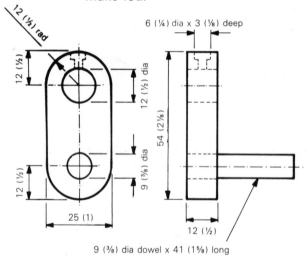

6 (¼) dia x 3 (⅛) deep

12 (½) rad

12 (½)

12 (½) dia

54 (2⅛)

9 (⅜) dia

12 (½)

25 (1)

12 (½)

9 (⅜) dia dowel x 41 (1⅝) long

3 (⅛) dia

Fig 37 Derrick post retaining collar
make four

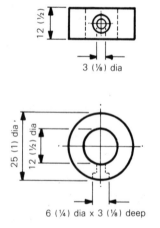

12 (½)

3 (⅛) dia

25 (1) dia

12 (½) dia

6 (¼) dia x 3 (⅛) deep

Fig 38 Deck block
make two

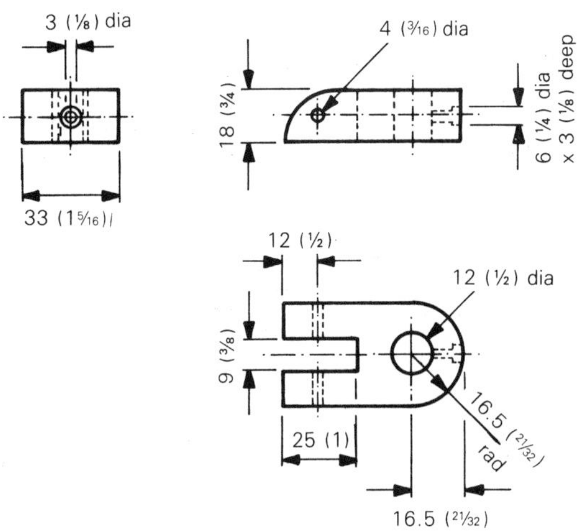

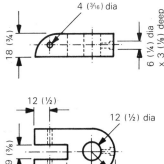

3 (⅛) dia

4 (³⁄₁₆) dia

18 (¾)

6 (¼) dia x 3 (⅛) deep

33 (1⁵⁄₁₆)

12 (½)

12 (½) dia

9 (³⁄₈)

25 (1)

16.5 (²¹⁄₃₂) rad

16.5 (²¹⁄₃₂)

Fig 39 Winch drum and handle assembly
make four

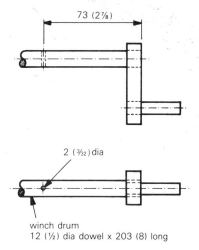

73 (2⅞)

2 (³⁄₃₂) dia

winch drum
12 (½) dia dowel x 203 (8) long

Fig 40 Derrick post
make two

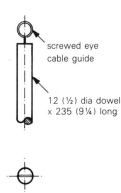

screwed eye
cable guide

12 (½) dia dowel
x 235 (9¼) long

Fig 41 Latch release rods
2 (³⁄₃₂) dia steel rod, make four

'X'

18 (¾)

Dimension 'X'
rod 'A' = 149 (5⅞)
rod 'B' = 46 (1¹³⁄₁₆)
rod 'C' = 67 (2⅝)
rod 'D' = 206 (8⅛)
see Fig 22 and 44 for assembly positions

33) in position centrally between the front, and rear body side panels (see also Fig 22). The appearance of the screw heads will be enhanced if cup washers are used.

26 Make the cogs (Fig 34), the latches (Fig 35), and the winch handle assemblies (Fig 36). Test assemble these parts (see Fig 22) with the winch drum assemblies (Fig 39).

27 Make the derrick post retaining collar (Fig 37), the deck blocks (Fig 38), the derrick posts (Fig 40), and the latch release rods (Fig 41).

28 Insert the parallel end of each boom into the slot of each deck block and secure using the deck block to boom connecting pins and spring dome caps.

29 Screw one pair of boom end plates (Fig 43) to each boom (Fig 42) using 9mm (⅜in) long, round head screws.

30 Insert one 4mm (³⁄₁₆in) dia steel rod 16mm (⅝in) long through the centre hole

Fig 42 Boom
make two

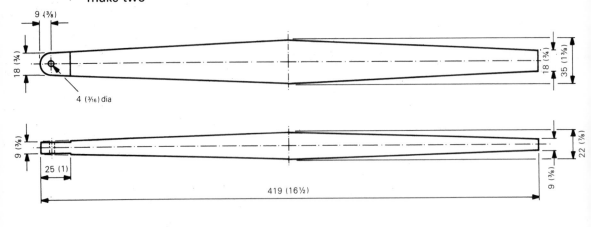

- 9 (⅜)
- 18 (¾)
- 4 (³⁄₁₆) dia
- 18 (¾)
- 35 (1⅜)
- 9 (⅜)
- 25 (1)
- 419 (16½)
- 22 (⅞)
- 9 (⅜)

Fig 43 Boom end plates
make two pairs, 1.5 (¹⁄₁₆) thick stainless steel

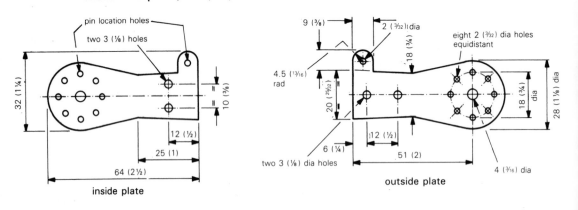

pin location holes

two 3 (⅛) holes

32 (1¼)

12 (½)

25 (1)

10 (⅜)

64 (2½)

inside plate

9 (⅜)

2 (³⁄₃₂) dia

eight 2 (³⁄₃₂) dia holes equidistant

4.5 (¹³⁄₁₆) rad

18 (¾)

20 (²⁵⁄₃₂)

18 (¾) dia

28 (1⅛) dia

12 (½)

6 (¼)

two 3 (⅛) dia holes

51 (2)

4 (³⁄₁₆) dia

outside plate

Spirit of America Wrecker Truck (page 112)

above Table (page 99), Chairs and Bench (page 102); *left* Toy Box (page 19), Hobby Horse (page 57); *right* Traffic Lights Game (page 88), Table Skittles (page 156)

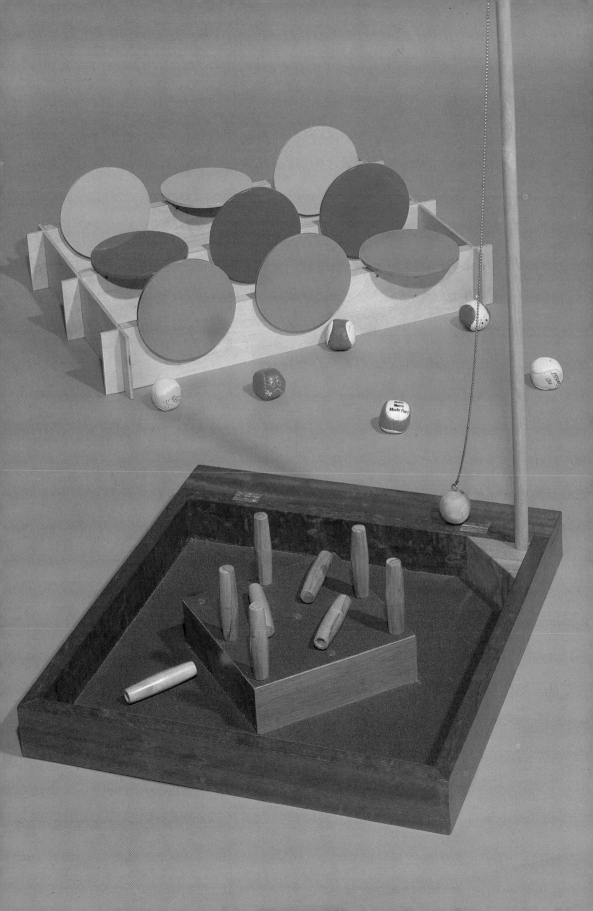

Fig 44 Goal-post cross-bar assembly

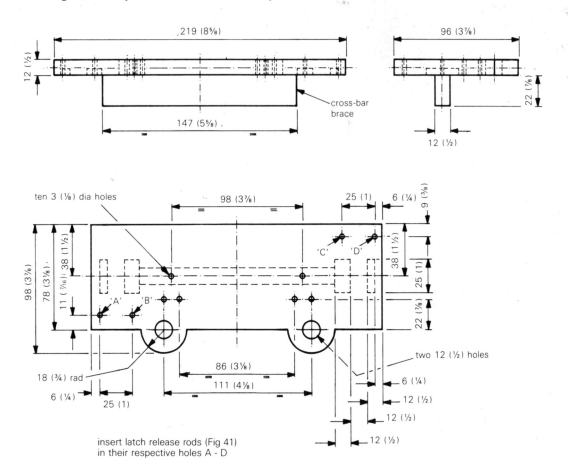

insert latch release rods (Fig 41)
in their respective holes A - D

Fig 45 Cross-bar brace
showing location positions of
rear goal-post support struts

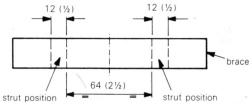

Dolls' Bunk Beds (page 92)

133

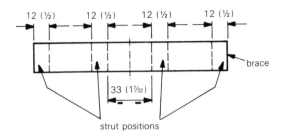

Fig 46 Cross-bar brace
showing location positions of
forward goal-post support struts

12 (½) 12 (½) 12 (½) 12 (½)

brace

33 (1⁷/₃₂)

strut positions

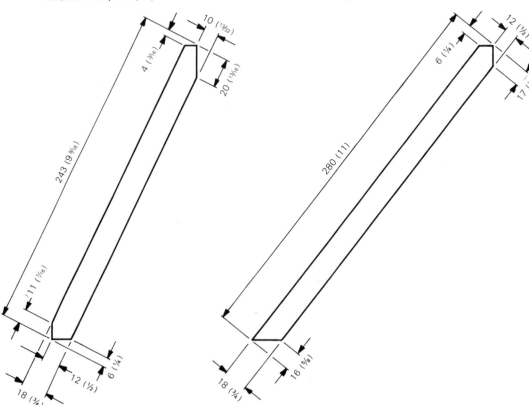

Fig 47 Forward goal-post support strut
make four, 12 (½) thick

10 (¹³/₃₂)

4 (³/₁₆)

20 (¹³/₁₆)

243 (9 ⁹/₁₆)

11 (⁷/₁₆)

12 (½)

6 (¼)

18 (¾)

Fig 48 Rear goal-post support strut
make two, 12 (½) thick

12 (½)

6 (¼)

17 (¹¹/₁₆)

280 (11)

18 (¾)

16 (⁵/₈)

of each boom end plate (Fig 43), and
secure using spring dome caps.
31 Insert one 2mm (³/₃₂in) dia steel rod
16mm (⁵/₈in) long through each boom end
plate pin locating hole (Fig 43), and
secure them using spring dome caps.
32 Cut out and make up the goal-post
cross-bar assembly (Fig 44). Extreme care
must be taken when cutting the outside

mortises, to avoid splitting the outer
faces.
33 Cut to length the latch pivot pins, and
fit the latches (Fig 35) in position (see Fig
22). *Note* The 2mm (³/₃₂in) dia hole of each
latch is the latch release rod location hole.
This location hole must be positioned
forward of the goal posts when assembling the right-hand latches, and reversed

Fig 49 Cab floor assembly
6 (¼) thick

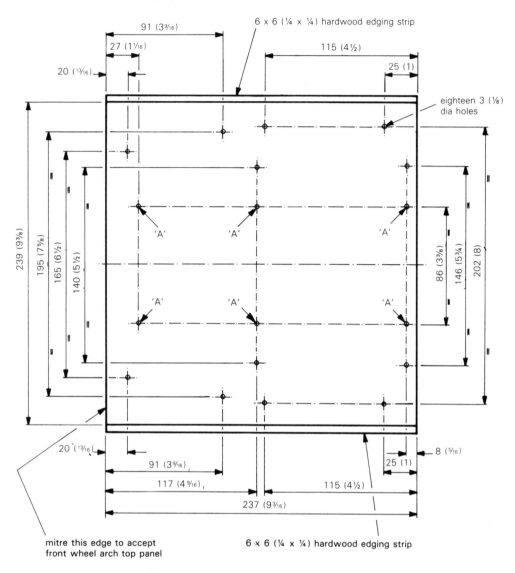

6 x 6 (¼ x ¼) hardwood edging strip

91 (3⁹⁄₁₆)

27 (1¹⁄₁₆)

115 (4½)

20 (¹³⁄₁₆)

25 (1)

eighteen 3 (⅛)
dia holes

239 (9⅜)

195 (7⅝)

165 (6½)

140 (5½)

'A'   'A'   'A'

'A'   'A'   'A'

86 (3⅜)

146 (5¾)

202 (8)

20 (¹³⁄₁₆)

91 (3⁹⁄₁₆)

117 (4⁹⁄₁₆)

115 (4½)

25 (1)

8 (⁵⁄₁₆)

237 (9³⁄₁₆)

mitre this edge to accept
front wheel arch top panel

6 x 6 (¼ x ¼) hardwood edging strip

csk holes 'A' on top face
csk all other holes on reverse face

Fig 50 Front wheel-arch assembly

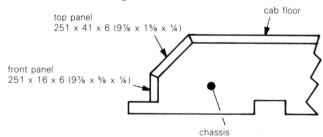

top panel
251 x 41 x 6 (9⅞ x 1⅝ x ¼)

cab floor

front panel
251 x 16 x 6 (9⅞ x ⅝ x ¼)

chassis

Fig 51 Cab floor assembly
showing cab walls, engine
compartment and seat positions

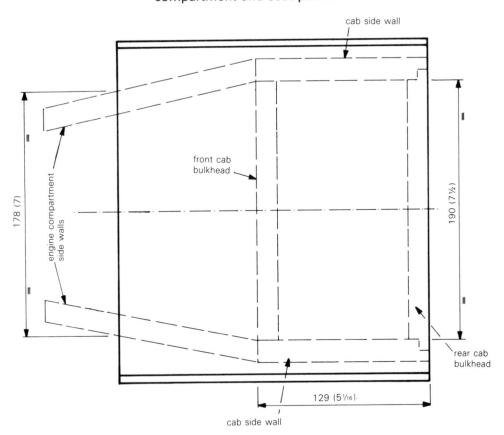

cab side wall

front cab
bulkhead

engine compartment
side walls

178 (7)

190 (7½)

rear cab
bulkhead

129 (5⅟₁₆)

cab side wall

for the left-hand latches.

34 Before fitting the goal-post cross bar in
position, insert each latch release rod into
its corresponding latch (Fig 44), and
secure using spring dome caps. Insert the
latch release rods into the goal-post cross
bar as it is being lowered into position.

35 Assemble winch drums, cogs and
winch handles as shown in Fig 22. Ensure
that cogs face a direction which enables
them to mesh with their partner latch.
Before screwing these parts in position,
drill pilot holes for each part into the
winch drums.

36 Place compression springs in position
(Fig 22) over the latch release rods, and
secure them with spring dome caps.
Springs should be of sufficient strength to
hold the latches tight against the cogs and

prevent reverse movement of the winch
drum. Do not coat the cog faces with
varnish, or teak oil. When fitting the
spring dome caps, hold them in place
using PVC tape and support the bottom
edge of each latch with a piece of scrap
wood.

If winch drums will not turn after
assembly, drums are either too tight in
the goal posts, or the lower point of the
latch is too sharp; ease as necessary. If a
cog is jamming inside the goal posts,
remove the cog and reduce its thickness
until it runs free.

37 Insert one derrick post through each
12mm (½in) dia hole in the goal-post
cross member, and assemble derrick posts
as shown in Fig 22. Locate the bottom of
each derrick post in the 12mm (½in) dia

Fig 52 Rear cab bulkhead

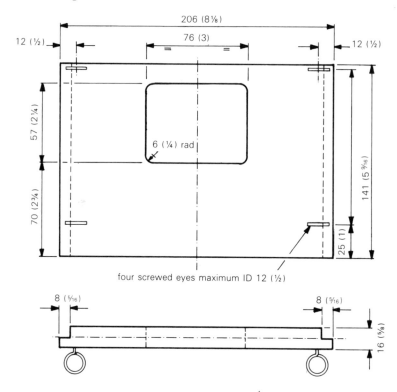

206 (8⅛)

76 (3)

12 (½)

12 (½)

57 (2¼)

6 (¼) rad

141 (5⁹⁄₁₆)

70 (2¾)

25 (1)

four screwed eyes maximum ID 12 (½)

8 (⁵⁄₁₆)

8 (⁵⁄₁₆)

16 (⅝)

Fig 53 Front cab bulkhead
16 (⅝) thick

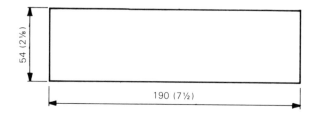

54 (2⅛)

190 (7½)

deck holes. Before screwing the deck blocks and derrick post retaining collars in position, drill pilot holes. Use teak oil to ease movement if required.

38 Glue the deck headboard (Fig 28) in position.

39 Make the goal-post support struts (Figs 47–8), and fit them in positions as shown in Figs 27–9, and Fig 45.

40 Glue the 6×6mm (¼×¼in) edging strip to the outer edges of the cab floor (Fig 49). Sand flush, then screw and glue the complete assembly in position.

41 Assemble the front wheel arch (Fig 50) onto the assembled chassis. Mitre edges as shown for an exact fit.

42 Cut out the rear cab bulkhead (Fig 52), the front cab bulkhead (Fig 53) and the cab side panels (Fig 54). When making the cab side panels (Fig 54), cut the outside shape before attempting to make the window opening. Drill pilot holes to accept each cab door handle. Dry assemble these parts before finally screwing

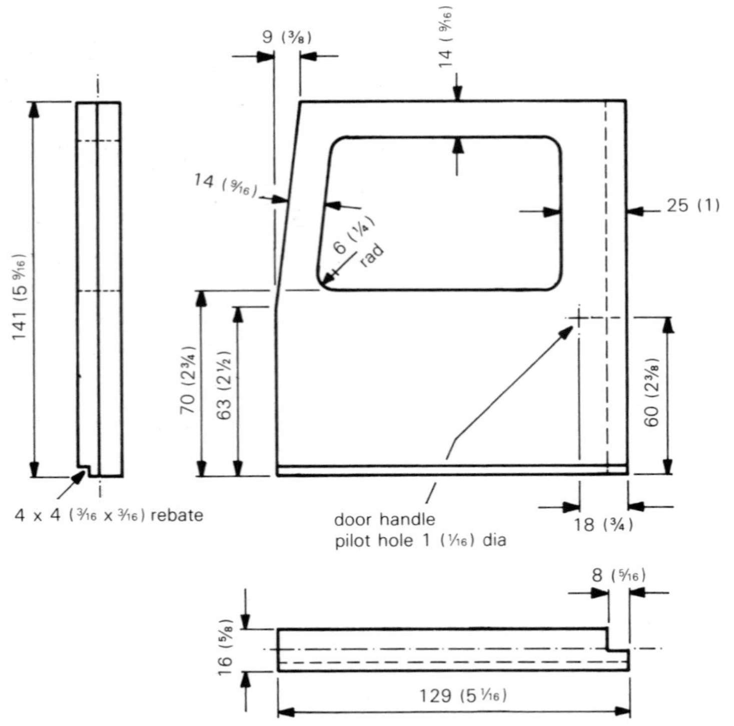

Fig 56 Engine compartment side panel
make one of each hand

58 (2¼)

167 (6⅝)

4 x 4 (³/₁₆ x ³/₁₆) rebate

110 (4⁵/₁₆)

25 (1)

87 (3 ⁷/₁₆)

16 (⅝)

3 (⅛)

chamfer to fit cab floor
and front wheel-arch assembly

3 (⅛)

Fig 54 Cab side panel
make one of each hand

25 (1)

60 (2⅜)

18 (¾)

14 (⁹/₁₆)

door handle
pilot hole 1 (¹/₁₆) dia

6 (¼)
rad

9 (⅜)

8 (⁵/₁₆)

129 (5 ¹/₁₆)

14 (⁹/₁₆)

63 (2½)

70 (2⅜)

16 (⅝)

141 (5 ⁹/₁₆)

4 x 4 (³/₁₆ x ³/₁₆) rebate

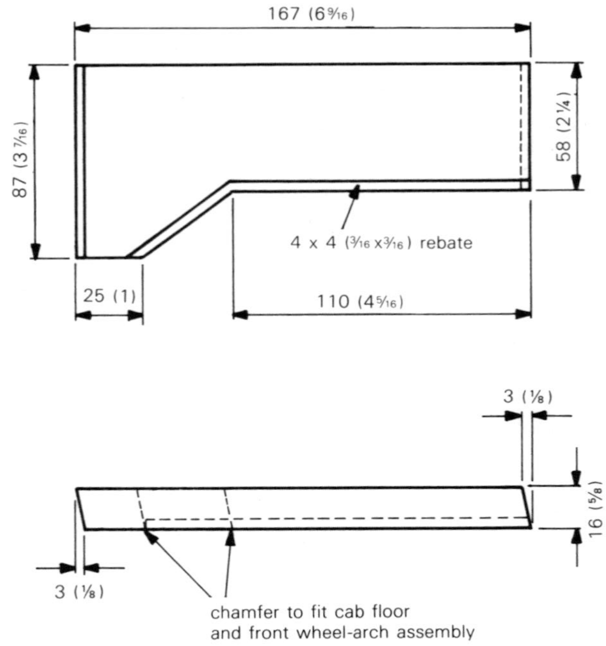

Fig 55 Door handle
make two using screwed eyes

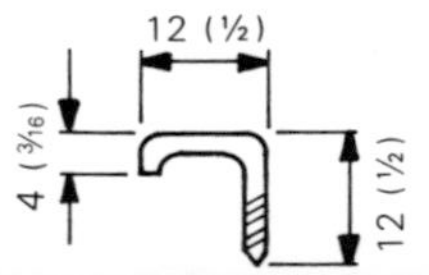

12 (½)

12 (½)

4 (³/₁₆)

Fig 57 Bonnet

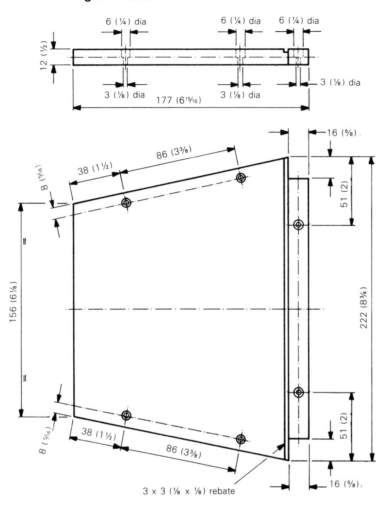

6 (¼) dia 6 (¼) dia 6 (¼) dia

12 (½)

3 (⅛) dia 177 (6¹⁵⁄₁₆) 3 (⅛) dia 3 (⅛) dia

16 (⅝)

86 (3³⁄₈)

38 (1½)

8 (⁵⁄₁₆)

51 (2)

156 (6⅛)

222 (8¾)

8 (⁵⁄₁₆)

38 (1½)

86 (3³⁄₈)

51 (2)

3 x 3 (⅛ x ⅛) rebate

16 (⅝)

also required: 4 off 6 (¼) dia x 6 (¼) long dowel plugs

and glueing them in position.

43 The engine compartment side panels have to be chamfered to fit at the required angle (see Fig 51). Do not remove too much material in between test fitting.

44 Screw and glue the bonnet (Fig 57) in position. Glue 6mm (¼in) long×6mm (¼in) dia dowel plugs in the screw holes and sand flush.

45 Make up the radiator grill assembly and screw and glue it in position. Screw heads can either be 'lost' as with the bonnet assembly, or made prominent using cup washers (see colour photo page 129). Shaping the radiator grill is best done when the complete assembly is in position, before the bumper is fitted.

46 Cut out the bumper (Fig 59) and glue it in position.

47 Shape, and glue in position the seats (Fig 60), and the dashboard assembly (Figs 61–2). The vehicle can be either right- or left-hand drive as required.

48 Carefully cut the windscreen (Fig 63) to size. Slide it into the 3×3mm (⅛×⅛in) bonnet rebate, then screw it to the cab side panels using roundhead screws.

49 Screw and glue the cab roof (Fig 64) in position. Glue 6mm (¼in) long×6mm (¼in) dia dowel plugs in the screw holes and sand flush.

50 Make up the exhaust stack assemblies

Fig 58 Radiator grill assembly

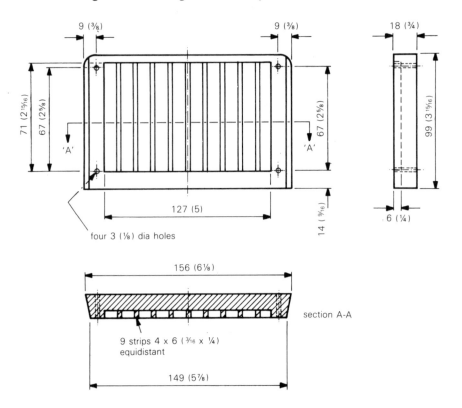

9 (³⁄₈)   9 (³⁄₈)   18 (¾)

71 (2¹⁵⁄₁₆)   67 (2⁵⁄₈)   'A'   67 (2⁵⁄₈)   'A'   99 (3¹⁵⁄₁₆)

127 (5)   14 (⁹⁄₁₆)   6 (¼)

four 3 (⅛) dia holes

156 (6⅛)

section A-A

9 strips 4 x 6 (³⁄₁₆ x ¼)
equidistant

149 (5⅞)

Fig 59 Bumper

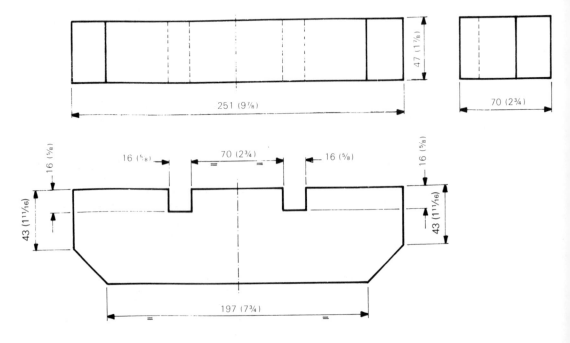

47 (1⅞)

251 (9⅞)   70 (2¾)

16 (⁵⁄₈)   16 (⁵⁄₈)   70 (2¾)   16 (⁵⁄₈)   16 (⁵⁄₈)

43 (1¹¹⁄₁₆)   43 (1¹¹⁄₁₆)

197 (7¾)

Fig 60 Seat
make two

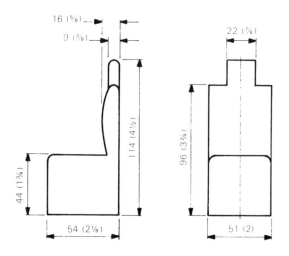

Fig 61 Dashboard

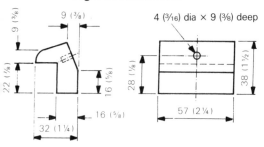

Fig 62 Steering-wheel assembly

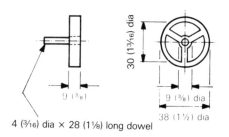

Fig 63 Windscreen
3 (⅛) thick perspex

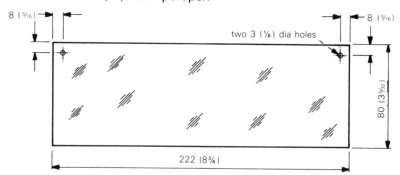

141

Fig 64 Cab roof

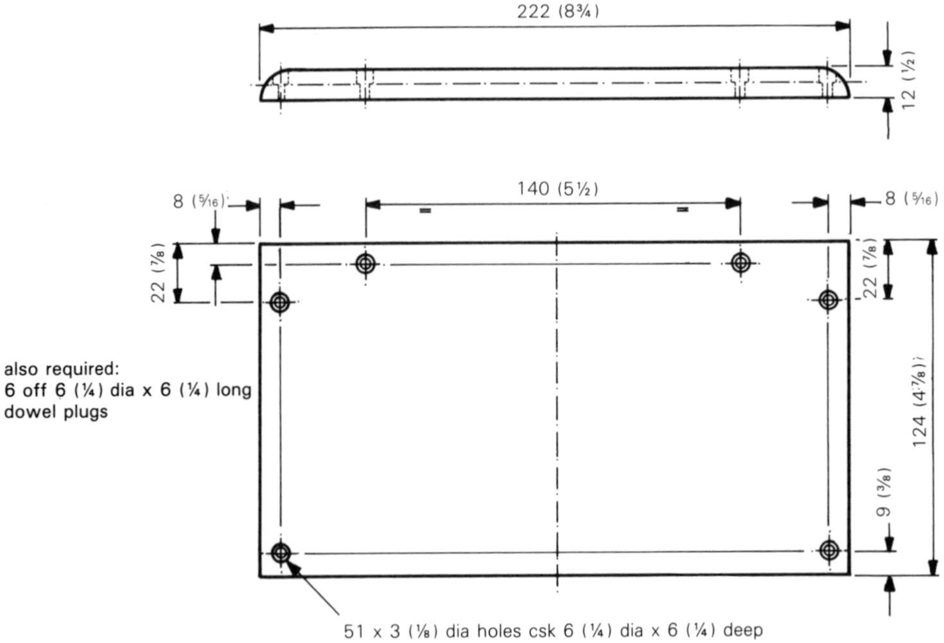

222 (8¾)
12 (½)
140 (5½)
8 (5⁄16)
8 (5⁄16)
22 (⅞)
22 (⅞)
124 (4⅞)
9 (⅜)
also required:
6 off 6 (¼) dia x 6 (¼) long
dowel plugs
51 x 3 (⅛) dia holes csk 6 (¼) dia x 6 (¼) deep

Fig 65 Exhaust stack
make two

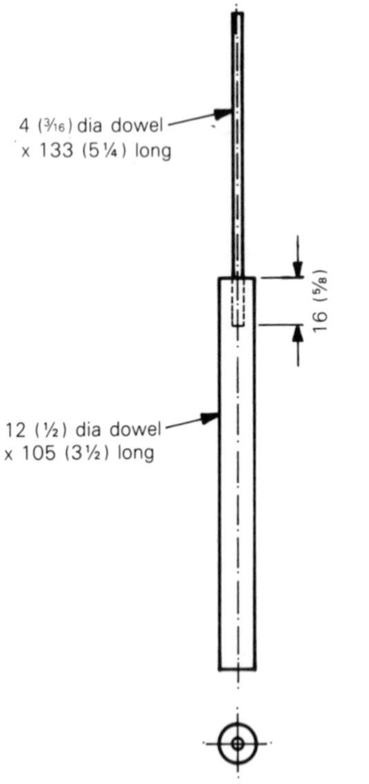

4 (3⁄16) dia dowel
x 133 (5¼) long
16 (⅝)
12 (½) dia dowel
x 105 (3½) long

Fig 66 Hook assembly
make two

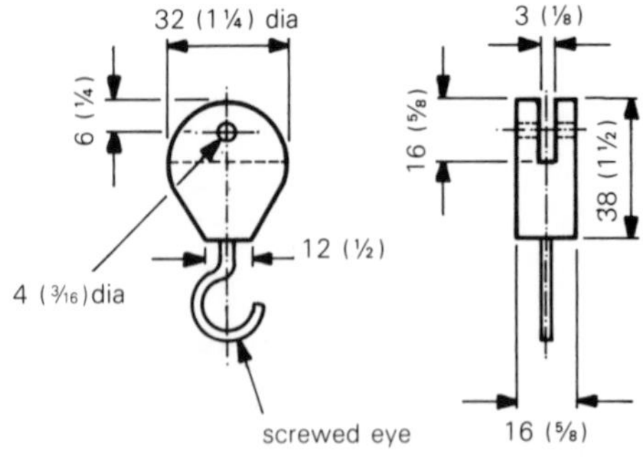

32 (1¼) dia
6 (¼)
12 (½)
4 (3⁄16)dia
screwed eye
3 (⅛)
16 (⅝)
38 (1½)
16 (⅝)

(Fig 65), and place them in position in the screwed eyes behind the rear cab bulkhead so that they are resting on the deck headboard. Squeeze the screwed eyes around the exhaust stacks to retain them.

51 Shape and make up the two hook assemblies (Fig 66). Insert a 22mm (⅞in) long×4mm (³⁄₁₆in) dia steel rod into each hook block and secure using spring dome caps. Use a large 22mm (⅞in) dia hook.

52 To rig the boom control cord, proceed as follows: Select the top winch drum of each pair, then pass a cord through its 2mm (³⁄₃₂in) dia hole and knot the end. Pass the free end of the cord up through the goal-post cross-bar hole which is directly in line with the derrick-post centre. Then pass the cord through the screwed eye in the derrick post and tie off on the inner 2mm (³⁄₃₂in) dia rod at the boom end plates. Use only cord which runs freely.

53 To rig the hook control, tie one end of your cord to an unused winch drum. Pass the free end through the goal-post cross bar and screwed eye. Pass it over the 4mm (³⁄₁₆in) dia rod at the boom end plates, and between the 4mm (³⁄₁₆in) dia hook rod and hook block. Take the cord back up and over the boom end rod and secure it on the inner 2mm (³⁄₃₂in) dia rod at the boom end plates.

Cutting list

Chassis longitudinal members (Fig 1)	2 off	772×57×16mm (30⅜×2¼×⅝in)	Wood
First and third cross members (Fig 4)	2 off	88×47×22mm (3½×1⅞×⅞in)	Wood
Second cross member (Fig 7)	1 off	102×59×22mm (4×2⁵⁄₁₆×⅞in)	Wood
Goal-post support members (Fig 8)	2 off	102×57×12mm (4×2¼×½in)	Wood
Fourth and fifth cross members (Fig 9)	2 off	235×57×16mm (9¼×2¼×⅝in)	Wood
Rear body panel (Fig 10)	1 off	235×63×22mm (9¼×2½×⅞in)	Wood
Rear bogie spacer blocks (Fig 11)	2 off	152×41×25mm (6×1⅝×1in)	Wood
Rear crash-bar supports (Fig 12)	2 off	57×25×16mm (2¼×1×⅝in)	Wood
Rear crash bar (Fig 13)	1 off	251mm (9⅞in) long 9mm (⅜in) dia dowel	
Rear wheel bogie (Fig 14)	2 off	152×67×16mm (6×2⅝×⅝in)	Wood
Front axle beams (Fig 15)	2 off	184×41×22mm (7¼×1⅝×⅞in)	Wood
Front axle blocks (Fig 17)	4 off	67×19×22mm (2⅝×¾×⅞in)	Wood
Steering tie bar (Fig 20)	2 off	184×18×12mm (7¼×¾×½in)	Wood
Steering bar (Fig 21)	1 off	381×22×12mm (15×⅞×½in)	Wood
Goal posts (Figs 23–6)	4 off	286×51×12mm (11¼×2×½in)	Wood
Deck (Fig 27)	1 off	478×235×6mm (10¹³⁄₁₆×9¼×¼in)	Plywood
Deck headboard (Fig 28)	1 off	219×15×16mm (8⅝×¹⁹⁄₃₂×⅝in)	Wood
Rear body side panels (Fig 30)	2 off	344×84×16mm (13⁹⁄₁₆×3⁵⁄₁₆×⅝in)	Wood
Grab rails (Fig 30)	2 off	263mm (10⁵⁄₁₆in) long×4mm (³⁄₁₆in) dia dowel	
Front body side panels (Fig 31)	2 off	116×72×16mm (4⁹⁄₁₆×2¼×⅝in)	Wood
Grab rails (Fig 31)	1 off	116mm (4⁹⁄₁₆in) long×4mm (³⁄₁₆in) dia dowel	
	1 off	97mm (3¹³⁄₁₆in) long×4mm (³⁄₁₆in) dia dowel	
Jacking legs (Fig 33)	2 off	67×12×12mm (2⅝×½×½in)	Wood
	2 off	25×18×3mm (1×¾×⅛in)	Wood
Cogs (Fig 34)	4 off	35mm (1⅜in) dia×11mm (⁷⁄₁₆in) thick	Wood

Latch (Fig 35)	4 off	48×16×11mm ($1\frac{7}{8}$×$\frac{5}{8}$×$\frac{7}{16}$in)	Wood
Winch handles (Fig 36)	4 off	54×25×12mm ($2\frac{1}{8}$×1×$\frac{1}{2}$in)	Wood
	4 off	41mm ($1\frac{5}{8}$in) long×9mm ($\frac{3}{8}$in) dia dowel	
Deck blocks (Fig 38)	2 off	60×33×18mm ($2\frac{3}{8}$×$1\frac{5}{16}$×$\frac{3}{4}$in)	Wood
Winch drums (Fig 39)	4 off	203mm (8in) long×12mm ($\frac{1}{2}$in) dia dowel	
Derrick posts (Fig 40)	2 off	235mm ($9\frac{1}{4}$in) long×12mm ($\frac{1}{2}$in) dia dowel	
Derrick post retaining collars (Fig 37)	2 off	25mm (1in) dia×12mm ($\frac{1}{2}$in) thick	Wood
Boom (Fig 42)	2 off	419×35×22mm ($16\frac{1}{2}$×$1\frac{3}{8}$×$\frac{7}{8}$in)	Wood
Goal-post cross bar (Fig 44)	1 off	219×96×12mm ($8\frac{5}{8}$×$3\frac{7}{8}$×$\frac{1}{2}$in)	Wood
Brace (Fig 44)	1 off	147×22×12mm ($5\frac{5}{8}$×$\frac{7}{8}$×$\frac{1}{2}$in)	Wood
Forward goal-post support struts (Fig 47)	4 off	243×18×12mm ($9\frac{9}{16}$×$\frac{3}{4}$×$\frac{1}{2}$in)	Wood
Rear goal-post support struts (Fig 48)	2 off	280×18×12mm (11×$\frac{3}{4}$×$\frac{1}{2}$in)	Wood
Cab floor (Fig 49)	1 off	237×239×6mm ($9\frac{3}{16}$×$9\frac{3}{8}$×$\frac{1}{4}$in)	Wood
edging strips	2 off	237×6×6mm ($9\frac{3}{16}$×$\frac{1}{4}$×$\frac{1}{4}$in)	Wood
Front wheel-arch top panel (Fig 50)	1 off	251×41×6mm ($9\frac{7}{8}$×$1\frac{5}{8}$×$\frac{1}{4}$in)	Plywood
Front wheel-arch front panel (Fig 50)	1 off	251×16×6mm ($9\frac{7}{8}$×$\frac{5}{8}$×$\frac{1}{4}$in)	Plywood
Rear cab bulkhead (Fig 52)	1 off	206×141×16mm ($8\frac{1}{8}$×$5\frac{9}{16}$×$\frac{5}{8}$in)	Wood
Front cab bulkhead (Fig 53)	1 off	190×54×16mm ($7\frac{1}{2}$×$2\frac{1}{8}$×$\frac{5}{8}$in)	Wood
Cab side panels (Fig 54)	2 off	129×141×16mm ($5\frac{1}{16}$×$5\frac{9}{16}$×$\frac{5}{8}$in)	Wood
Engine compartment side panels (Fig 56)	2 off	167×87×16mm ($6\frac{9}{16}$×$3\frac{7}{16}$×$\frac{5}{8}$in)	Wood
Bonnet (Fig 57)	1 off	177×222×16mm ($6\frac{15}{16}$×$8\frac{3}{4}$×$\frac{5}{8}$in)	Wood
dowel plugs (Fig 57)	6 off	6mm ($\frac{1}{4}$in) long×6mm ($\frac{1}{4}$in) dia dowel	
Radiator grill (Fig 58)	1 off	156×99×18mm ($6\frac{1}{8}$×$3\frac{15}{16}$×$\frac{3}{4}$in)	Wood
	9 off	4×6×71mm ($\frac{3}{16}$×$\frac{1}{4}$×$2\frac{13}{16}$in)	Wood
Bumper (Fig 59)	1 off	251×70×47mm ($9\frac{7}{8}$×$2\frac{3}{4}$×$1\frac{7}{8}$in)	Wood
Seats (Fig 60)	2 off	54×114×51mm ($2\frac{1}{8}$×$4\frac{1}{2}$×2in)	Wood
Dashboard (Fig 61)	1 off	57×38×32mm ($2\frac{1}{4}$×$1\frac{1}{2}$×$1\frac{1}{4}$in)	Wood
Steering wheel (Fig 62)	1 off	38mm ($1\frac{1}{2}$in) dia×9mm ($\frac{3}{8}$in) thick	Wood
Steering column (Fig 62)	1 off	28mm ($1\frac{1}{8}$in) long×4mm ($\frac{3}{16}$in) dia dowel	
Cab roof (Fig 64)	1 off	222×124×12mm ($8\frac{3}{4}$×$4\frac{7}{8}$×$\frac{1}{2}$in)	Wood
dowel plugs (Fig 64)	6 off	6mm ($\frac{1}{4}$in) long×6mm ($\frac{1}{4}$in) dia dowel	
Exhaust stacks (Fig 65)	2 off	133mm ($5\frac{1}{4}$in) long×4mm ($\frac{3}{16}$in) dia dowel	
	2 off	105mm ($3\frac{1}{2}$in) long×12mm ($\frac{1}{2}$in) dia dowel	
Hooks (Fig 66)	2 off	32×38×16mm ($1\frac{1}{4}$×$1\frac{1}{2}$×$\frac{5}{8}$in)	Wood

Ancillaries

Front wheel pivot plates (Fig 5)	4 off	45×50×1.5mm ($1\frac{3}{4}$×2×$\frac{1}{16}$in) Stainless steel
Front axle beam pivot pins	2 off	35mm ($1\frac{3}{8}$in) long×6mm ($\frac{1}{4}$in) dia steel rod
spring dome caps	4 off	to suit 6mm ($\frac{1}{4}$in) dia steel rod
Rear crash bar	2 off	12mm ($\frac{1}{2}$in) dia screwed eyes
Rear wheel bogie pivot rod	1 off	226mm ($8\frac{7}{8}$in) long×6mm ($\frac{1}{4}$in) dia steel rod
spring dome caps	2 off	to suit 6mm ($\frac{1}{4}$in) dia steel rod
Rear axles	2 off	257mm ($10\frac{1}{8}$in) long×6mm ($\frac{1}{4}$in) dia steel rod
spring dome caps	4 off	to suit 6mm ($\frac{1}{4}$in) dia steel rod
flat washers	4 off	inside dia 6mm ($\frac{1}{4}$in)

Front and rear wheels	8 off	102mm (4in) dia axle size 6mm (¼in) dia
Steering plates (Figs 18 and 19)	4 off	41×22×1.5mm (1⅝×⅞×¹⁄₁₆in) Stainless steel
Front axle block pivot pins	4 off	49mm (1¹⁵⁄₁₇in) long×4mm (³⁄₁₆in) dia steel rod
spring dome caps	8 off	to suit 4mm (³⁄₁₆in) dia rod
Stub axles	4 off	64mm (2½in) long×6mm (¼in) dia steel rod
flat washers	4 off	inside dia 6mm (¼in)
spring dome caps	8 off	to suit 6mm (¼in) dia rod
Front axle block to steering tie bar connecting pins	4 off	38mm (1½in) long×4mm (³⁄₁₆in) dia steel rod
spring dome caps	8 off	to suit 4mm (³⁄₁₆in) dia rod
Steering bar to steering tie bar connecting pins	2 off	35mm (1⅜in) long×4mm (³⁄₁₆in) dia steel rod
spring dome caps	4 off	to suit 4mm (³⁄₁₆in) dia rod
Steering bar to second cross member connecting pin	1 off	43mm (1¹¹⁄₁₆in) long×4mm (³⁄₁₆in) dia steel rod
spring dome caps	2 off	to suit 4mm (³⁄₁₆in) dia rod
Rear body side panel grab rail retaining eyes	6 off	12mm (½in) dia screwed eyes
Front body side panel grab rail retaining eyes	4 off	12mm (½in) dia screwed eyes
Ladder (Fig 32)	2 off	67×35×1.5mm (2⅝×1⅜×¹⁄₁₆in) Stainless steel
Latch pivot pins (Fig 22)	4 off	36mm (1½in) long×3mm (⅛in) dia steel rod
Deck block flat washers (Fig 22)	2 off	inside dia 12mm (½in)
Deck block to boom connecting pin	2 off	41mm (1⅝in) long×4mm (³⁄₁₆in) dia steel rod
spring dome caps	4 off	to suit 4mm (³⁄₁₆in) dia rod
Derrick post cable guide (Fig 40)	2 off	12mm (½in) dia screwed eyes
Latch release rods (Fig 41)		
rod 'A'	1 off	149mm (5⅞in) long×2mm (³⁄₃₂in) dia steel rod
rod 'B'	1 off	46mm (1¹³⁄₁₆in) long×2mm (³⁄₃₂in) dia steel rod
rod 'C'	1 off	67mm (2⅝in) long×2mm (³⁄₃₂in) dia steel rod
rod 'D'	1 off	206mm (8⅛in) long×2mm (³⁄₃₂in) dia steel rod
	4 off	16mm (⅝in) long×6mm (¼in) dia compression springs
spring dome caps	16 off	to suit 2mm (³⁄₃₂in) dia rod
Boom end plates (Fig 43)	4 off	64×32×1.5mm (2½×1¼×¹⁄₁₆in) Stainless steel
	4 off	16mm (⅝in) long×2mm (³⁄₃₂in) dia steel rod
spring dome caps	8 off	to suit 2mm (³⁄₃₂in) dia rod
	2 off	16mm (⅝in) long×4mm (³⁄₁₆in) dia steel rod
spring dome caps	4 off	to suit 4mm (³⁄₁₆in) dia rod
Rear cab bulkhead (Fig 52)	4 off	screwed eyes 12mm (½in) dia
Cab door handle (Fig 55)	2 off	12mm (½in) dia screwed eyes
Windscreen (Fig 63)	1 off	222×80×3mm (8¾×3⁵⁄₃₂×⅛in) Clear perspex
Hooks (Fig 66)	2 off	22mm (⅞in) dia screwed eyes
	2 off	22mm (⅞in) long×4mm (³⁄₁₆in) dia steel rod
spring dome caps	4 off	to suit 4mm (³⁄₁₆in) dia rod

SIT 'N RIDE FIRE ENGINE

Children are enthralled by fire engines racing down the high street with their sirens wailing and lights flashing. A child's dream is turned into reality as he drives his own fire engine to the rescue.

Battery-operated accessories available for bicycles which give electronic fire, police and ambulance sounds can be added, fitted inside the vehicle on the chassis.

1 Cut the four longitudinal chassis members to length, and assemble (Fig 1).

2 Mark onto each chassis member the positions of the axle beam stops (Figs 1 and 2). Drill and countersink two fixing holes through each chassis member, then screw and glue the stops in position.

3 Screw and glue the cross member (Fig 3) in position (Figs 1 and 2).

4 Assemble the rear axle beam (Fig 4) using hardwood for the axle blocks. Screw and glue the completed assembly in position (Figs 1 and 2).

5 Screw and glue one steering plate (Fig 5) to the assembled chassis (Figs 1 and 2).

6 Cut out two blind mortises in the front bulkhead (Fig 6). Test assemble onto the chassis (Fig 2). When blind mortises are completed, screw and glue two spacer blocks to the front bulkhead.

7 Mark the position of the completed front bulkhead assembly (Fig 6) onto the front bumper (Fig 7). Screw and glue the two parts together.

8 Screw and glue the assembled front bulkhead and bumper to the chassis (Fig 2).

9 In order, screw and glue the first, second, third and fourth formers (Figs 8, 9, 10 and 11) to the chassis assembly (Fig 2). Use a straight edge across the formers to ensure correct alignment before fitting plywood body panels. Chamfer the bottom edge of the fourth former to fit flush with the underbody panel (Figs 12 and 14).

10 The underbody panel (Fig 12) is now screwed and glued in position (Fig 14).

11 Drill two 4mm (³⁄₁₆in) dia fixing holes in the rear bumper (Fig 13), then screw and glue it in position (Fig 14).

12 Assemble the front axle beam (Fig 15).

As with the rear axle beam assembly, hardwood should be used to make the axle blocks.

13 Mark and cut out the steering wheel (Figs 16 and 17). Smooth off all edges.

14 Cut out two lower side panels (Fig 18). Place them in position across the formers, marking the location of each former on the inside face. Exchange the left-hand panel for the right-hand panel so that the marked areas are now facing outward. Drill and countersink two 3mm (⅛in) dia fixing holes along the centre line of each marked area, then screw and glue both panels in position.

15 Fit top side panels (Fig 19) in the same way as lower side panels.

16 Cut to size the front panel (Fig 20). Fit in position and chamfer both top and bottom edges for a good fit before finally glueing in place.

17 Place the top panel (Fig 21) in position and mark on its underside the location of the formers. Drill and countersink three 3mm (⅛in) dia fixing holes along the centre line of each marked area. Screw and glue panel in position.

18 Cut the steering column to length (see Cutting List). Drill a 4mm (³⁄₁₆in) dia hole, 25mm (1in) from the top end.

19 Screw and glue the bottom end of the steering column into the front axle beam (Fig 15).

20 Pass the steering column through the fixed steering plate which is attached to the chassis, and continue through the hole in the top panel. Place a flat washer with an inside diameter of 18mm (¾in) over the protruding steering column, then place the steering wheel onto the column.

21 Cut the retaining collar pin to length, fitting a spring dome cap to one end. Insert the pin into the retaining collar through the steering column and secure using another spring dome cap.

22 Insert axles into axle blocks, fit wheels placing a flat washer between wheel and axle block.

23 Fill all screw holes with a non-toxic filler, sand down and paint.

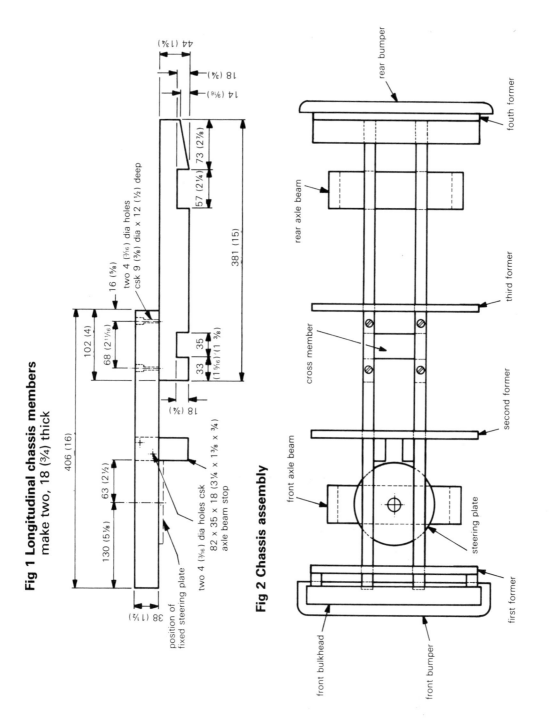

Fig 1 Longitudinal chassis members
make two, 18 (3/4) thick

two 4 (3/16) dia holes
csk 9 (3/8) dia x 12 (1/2) deep

two 4 (3/16) dia holes csk
82 x 35 x 18 (3¼ x 1⅜ x ¾)
axle beam stop

position of
fixed steering plate

406 (16)

130 (5⅛)

63 (2½)

102 (4)

68 (2¹¹/₁₆)

16 (⅝)

38 (1½)

18 (⅞)

381 (15)

57 (2¼)

73 (2⅞)

35

33
(1⁵/₁₆) (1 ⅜)

44 (1¾)

18 (¾)

14 (⁹/₁₆)

Fig 2 Chassis assembly

rear bumper

fouth former

rear axle beam

third former

cross member

second former

front axle beam

steering plate

first former

front bulkhead

front bumper

147

Fig 3 Cross member
18 (¾) thick

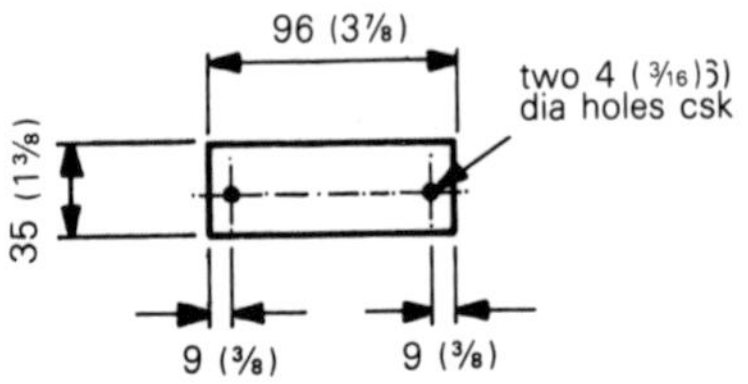

96 (3⅞)

35 (1⅜)

two 4 (³⁄₁₆)5)
dia holes csk

9 (⅜)   9 (⅜)

Fig 4 Rear axle beam assembly

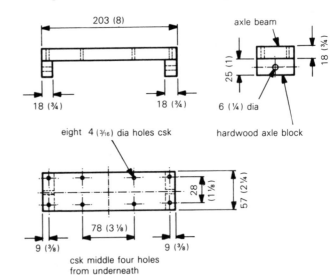

203 (8)

axle beam

25 (1)

18 (¾)

6 (¼) dia

18 (¾)   18 (¾)

eight 4 (³⁄₁₆) dia holes csk

hardwood axle block

28 (1⅛)

57 (2¼)

78 (3⅛)

9 (⅜)   9 (⅜)

csk middle four holes
from underneath

Fig 5 Steering plates
make two, 12 (½) thick

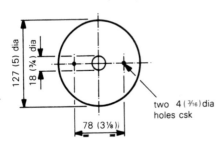

127 (5) dia

18 (¾) dia

two 4 (³⁄₁₆) dia
holes csk

78 (3⅛)

Fig 6 Front bulkhead assembly

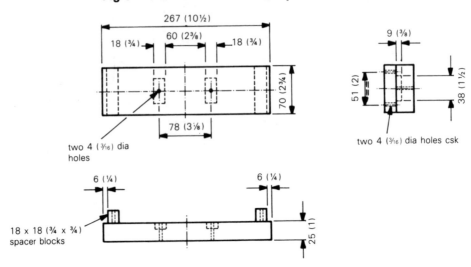

267 (10½)

60 (2⅜)

18 (¾)   18 (¾)

70 (2¾)

51 (2)

9 (⅜)

38 (1½)

78 (3⅛)

two 4 (³⁄₁₆) dia
holes

two 4 (³⁄₁₆) dia holes csk

6 (¼)   6 (¼)

18 x 18 (¾ x ¾)
spacer blocks

25 (1)

148

Fig 7 Front bumper

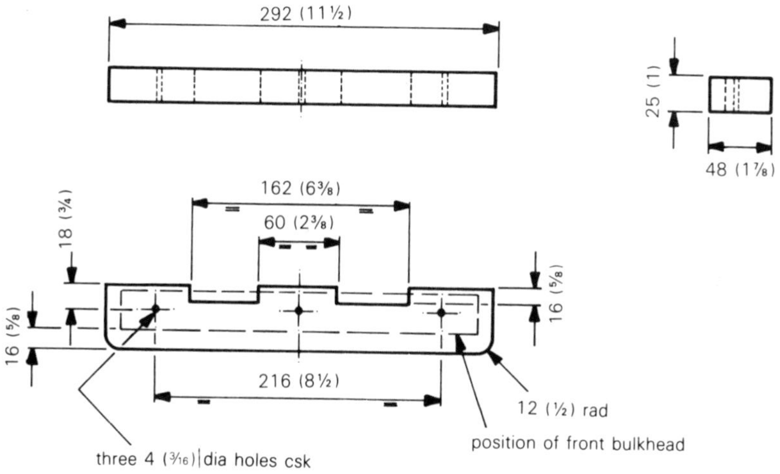
292 (11½)
25 (1)
48 (1⅞)
162 (6⅜)
60 (2⅜)
18 (¾)
16 (⅝)
16 (⅝)
216 (8½)
12 (½) rad
position of front bulkhead
three 4 (3/16) dia holes csk

Fig 8 First former
12 (½) thick

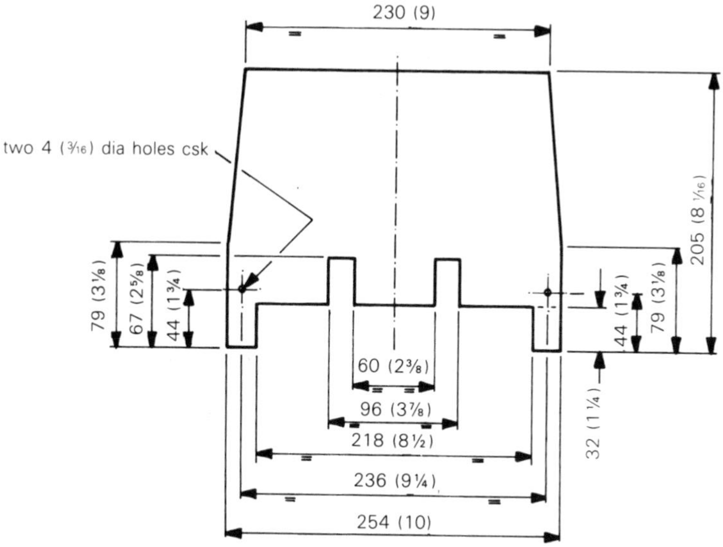
230 (9)
two 4 (3/16) dia holes csk
205 (8 1/16)
79 (3⅛)
67 (2⅝)
44 (1¾)
44 (1¾)
79 (3⅛)
32 (1¼)
60 (2⅜)
96 (3⅞)
218 (8½)
236 (9¼)
254 (10)

Fig 9 Second former
12 (½) thick

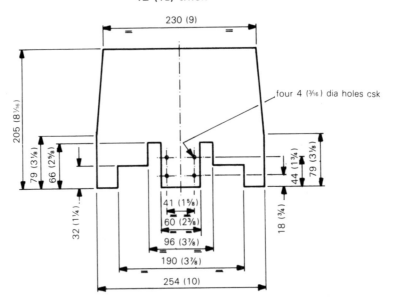

230 (9)

four 4 (³⁄₁₆) dia holes csk

205 (8¹⁄₁₆)
79 (3⅛)
66 (2⅝)
44 (1¾)
79 (3⅛)
32 (1¼)
41 (1⅝)
60 (2⅜)
96 (3⅞)
18 (¾)
190 (3⅞)
254 (10)

Fig 10 Third former
12 (½) thick

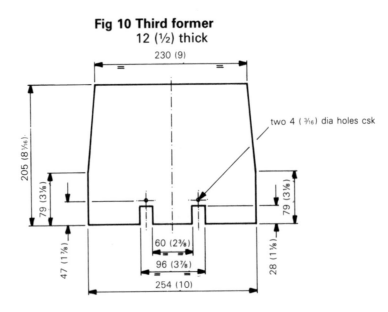

230 (9)

two 4 (³⁄₁₆) dia holes csk

205 (8¹⁄₁₆)
79 (3⅛)
79 (3⅛)
47 (1⅞)
60 (2⅜)
96 (3⅞)
28 (1⅛)
254 (10)

Fig 11 Fourth former assembly

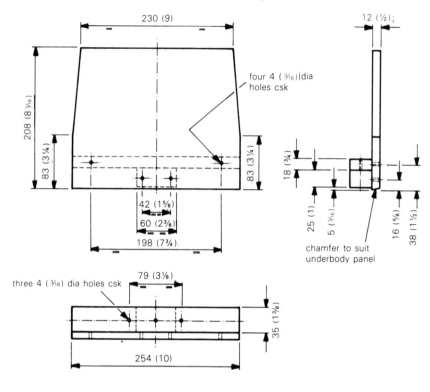

230 (9)

12 (½);

208 (8 3/16)

83 (3¼)

four 4 (3/16)ídia holes csk

83 (3¼)

42 (1⅝)

60 (2⅜)

198 (7¾)

18 (¾)

25 (1)

5 (3/16)

16 (⅝)

38 (1½)

chamfer to suit underbody panel

three 4 (3/16) dia holes csk

79 (3⅛)

35 (1⅜)

254 (10)

Fig 12 Underbody panel
6 (¼) thick

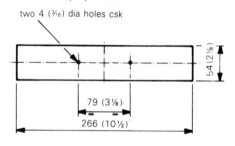

two 4 (3/16) dia holes csk

54 (2⅛)

79 (3⅛)

266 (10½)

Fig 14 Fixing position of underbody panel

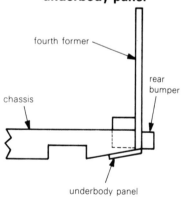

fourth former

rear bumper

chassis

underbody panel

Fig 13 Rear bumper
25 (1) thick

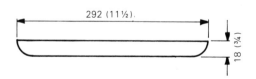

292 (11½)

18 (¾)

151

Fig 15 Front axle beam assembly

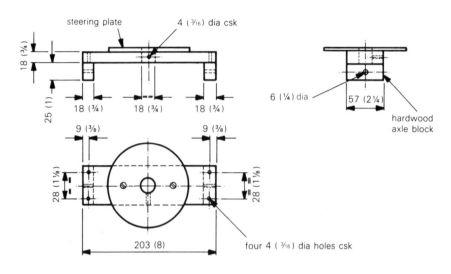

steering plate

4 (³⁄₁₆) dia csk

18 (¾)

25 (1)

18 (¾) 18 (¾) 18 (¾)

6 (¼) dia   57 (2¼)

hardwood
axle block

9 (⅜)   9 (⅜)

28 (1⅛)   28 (1⅛)

203 (8)   four 4 (³⁄₁₆) dia holes csk

Fig 16 Steering wheel assembly

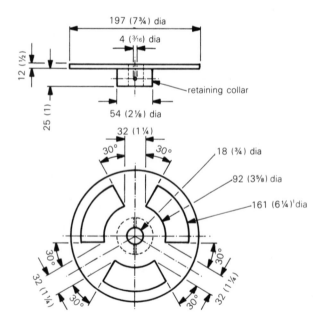

197 (7¾) dia

4 (³⁄₁₆) dia

12 (½)

25 (1)

retaining collar

54 (2⅛) dia

32 (1¼)

30°   30°

18 (¾) dia

92 (3⅝) dia

161 (6¼)'dia

30°

32 (1¼)

30°

30°   32 (1¼)

30°

Fig 17 Steering wheel drilling detail

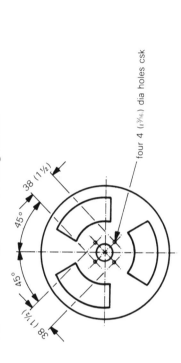

45°
38 (1½)
45°
38 (1½)
four 4 (³⁄₁₆) dia holes csk

Fig 18 Lower side panels
make two, 6 (¼) thick

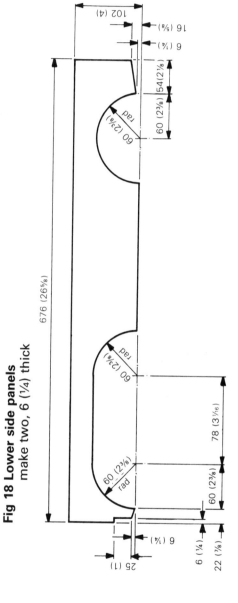

102 (4)
16 (⁵⁄₈)
6 (¼)
54 (2⅛)
60 (2³⁄₈)
60 (2³⁄₈) rad
676 (26⁵⁄₈)
60 (2³⁄₈) rad
78 (3¹⁄₁₆)
60 (2³⁄₈) rad
60 (2³⁄₈)
6 (¼)
9
22 (⁷⁄₈)
25 (1)

Fig 19 Top side panel
make two, 6 (¼) thick

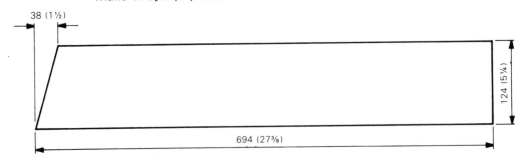

38 (1½)

124 (5¼)

694 (27⅜)

Fig 20 Front panel
6 (¼) thick

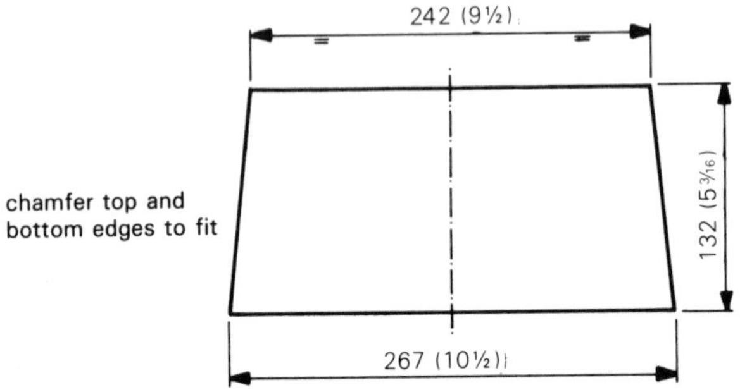

242 (9½)

132 (5 3⁄16)

chamfer top and
bottom edges to fit

267 (10½)

Fig 21 Top panel
6 (¼) thick

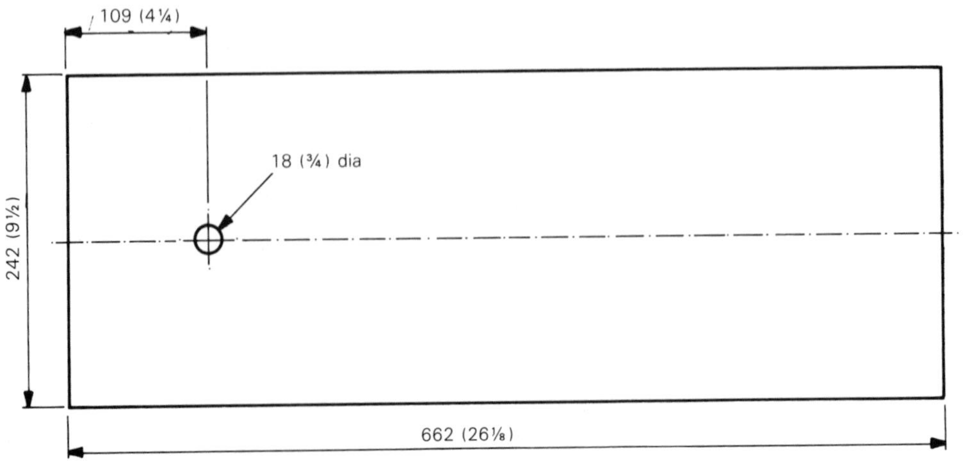

109 (4¼)

18 (¾) dia

242 (9½)

662 (26⅛)

Cutting list

Longitudinal chassis members (Fig 1)	2 off	406×38×18mm (16×1½×¾in)	Wood
	2 off	381×44×18mm (15×1¾×¾in)	Wood
Steering stops (Fig 1)	2 off	82×35×18mm (3¼×1⅜×¾in)	Wood
Cross member (Figs 1 and 3)	1 off	96×35×18mm (3⅞×1⅜×¾in)	Wood
Rear and front axle beams (Figs 4 and 15)	1 off	each 203×57×18mm (8×2¼×¾in)	Wood
Axle blocks (Figs 4 and 15)	4 off	57×25×18mm (2¼×1×¾in)	Hardwood
Steering plates (Figs 1, 5 and 15)	2 off	127mm (5in) dia×12mm (½in) thick	Plywood
Front bulkhead (Fig 6)	1 off	267×70×25mm (10½×2¾×1in)	Wood
Spacer blocks (Fig 6)	2 off	70×18×18mm (2¾×¾×¾in)	Wood
Front bumper (Fig 7)	1 off	292×48×25mm (11½×1⅞×1in)	Wood
First, second & third formers (Figs 8, 9 and 10)	1 off	each 254×205×6mm (10×8¹⁄₁₆×¼in)	Plywood
Fourth former (Fig 11)	1 off	254×208×6mm (10×8³⁄₁₆×¼in)	Plywood
	1 off	254×35×18mm (10×1⅜×¾in)	Wood
	1 off	60×35×18mm (2⅜×1⅜×¾in)	Wood
Underbody panel (Fig 12)	1 off	266×54×6mm (10½×2⅛×¼in)	Plywood
Rear bumper (Fig 13)	1 off	292×25×18mm (11½×1×¾in)	Wood
Steering wheel (Figs 16 and 17)	1 off	197mm (7¾in) dia×12mm (½in) thick	Plywood
Retaining collar (Fig 16)	1 off	54mm (2⅛in) dia×25mm (1in) thick	Wood
Lower side panels (Fig 18)	2 off	676×102×6mm (26⅝×4×¼in)	Plywood
Top side panels (Fig 19)	2 off	694×124×6mm (27⅜×5¼×¼in)	Plywood
Front panel (Fig 20)	1 off	267×132×6mm (10½×5³⁄₁₆×¼in)	Plywood
Top panel (Fig 21)	1 off	662×242×6mm (26⅛×9½×¼in)	Plywood
Steering column	1 off	264mm (10½in) long×18mm (¾in) dia dowel	

Ancillaries

Axles	2 off	277mm (10¹⁵⁄₁₆in) long×6mm (¼in) dia steel rod
spring dome caps	4 off	to suit 6mm (¼in) dia rod
flat washers	4 off	inside dia 6mm (¼in)
Retaining collar pin	1 off	65mm (2⅝in) long×4mm (³⁄₁₆in) dia steel rod
spring dome caps	2 off	to suit 4mm (³⁄₁₆in) dia rod
flat washer	1 off	inside dia 18mm (¾in)
Wheels	4 off	102mm (4in) dia – axle size 6mm (¼in) dia

TABLE SKITTLES
(DEVIL AMONG THE TAILORS)

The game of Table Skittles, or to use its traditional name, 'Devil Among the Tailors', is a pub game which originated in London in 1783. How it got its name is not a documented fact, but with the facts that are available it is believed to have come about when the tailors of London congregated at the Haymarket Theatre to protest about a play called *The Tailors: A Tragedy For Warm Weather*.

The tailors thought the play was insulting to their trade, and as a result of their enthusiastic protests, a riot broke out. The association between the game and the tailors could be related to the way in which the tailors were knocked down as the riot was controlled. An expression still in use today 'going down like nine pins'

probably relates to the 1783 tailors and the nine pins used in this game.

Table Skittles is an exciting game for all the family. A player's lead can be eroded instantly with one good score from an opponent. To play the game, the chain supporting the wooden ball is gently pulled straight. The ball is then swung around the pole in the direction shown in Fig 1, and will hopefully knock down a few skittles in the process.

Thirty-one Up
This variation is a standard game and the first player to knock down thirty-one skittles, finishing on the exact number of skittles required to make thirty-one, is the winner.

Fig 1 Assembled table

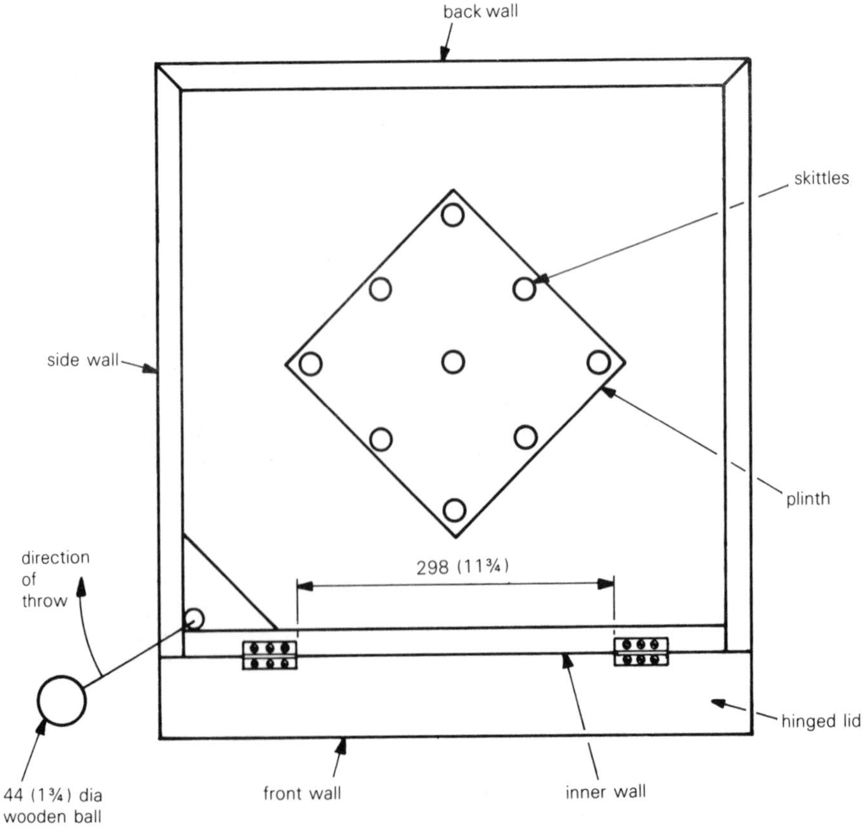

44 (1¾) dia wooden ball · front wall · inner wall · direction of throw · 298 (11¾) · side wall · back wall · skittles · plinth · hinged lid

Fig 2 Back wall

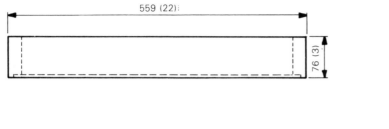

559 (22)

76 (3)

25 (1)

6 (¼)

17 (¹¹⁄₁₆)

45°   45°

Fig 3 Side walls
make one of each hand

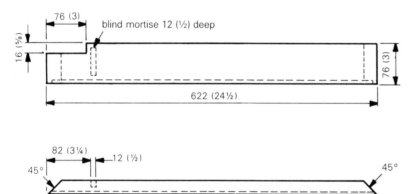

76 (3)

blind mortise 12 (½) deep

16 (⅝)

622 (24½)

76 (3)

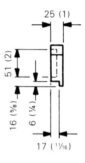

25 (1)

51 (2)

16 (⅝)

6 (¼)

17 (¹¹⁄₁₆)

82 (3¼)

12 (½)

45°   45°

Fives and Threes

In this game only skittles knocked down in multiples of five and three count towards any score. A score of five or three skittles knocked down counts as one point. Six or ten skittles count as two points and so on. Fifteen skittles count as eight points because fifteen is a multiple of both numbers.

Scoring for both these games, and any others you may like to invent, can easily be kept using a cribbage board. When play has finished, the skittles can be kept together in the storage compartment at the front of the table.

1 As can be seen from the drawings, the base (Fig 6) is fitted inside a rebate that runs around the inside edge of each outer wall. However, if you do not have equipment capable of producing these rebates, proceed as follows:

a) Reduce the height of the back wall (Fig 2), the side walls (Fig 3) and the front wall (Fig 5) by 6mm (¼in).

b) Increase the base length and width by 16mm (⅝in).

c) Reduce the height of the plinth walls (Fig 7) by 12mm (½in).

d) Increase the length and width of the plinth top (Fig 8) by 16mm (⅝in).

157

Fig 4 Inner wall

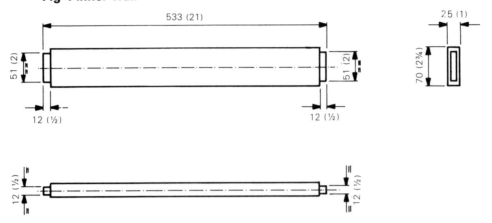

Fig 5 Front wall

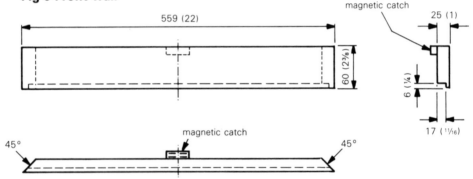

With these alterations the walls will fit flush to the edge of the base.

2 Make the back wall (Fig 2), the side walls (Fig 3), the inner wall (Fig 4) and the front wall (Fig 5). Screw a magnetic catch to the front wall (Fig 5) before final assembly.

3 Mark the hinge positions (see Fig 1) on the inner wall (Fig 4). Screw both hinges in position and mark around each one using a sharp trimming knife. Remove hinges, then remove sufficient wood from the marked areas to enable each hinge to fit flush with the top face of the wall. Screw each hinge in position.

4 Cut out the base (Fig 6).

5 Dry assemble the walls onto the base as shown in Fig 1.

6 Mark around the walls onto the base with a pencil. Remove the walls and drill suitable fixing holes, not forgetting the inner wall.

7 Make the plinth walls (Fig 7) and the plinth top (Fig 8). Place the walls inverted onto the plinth top and mark their position. Drill suitable fixing holes, then screw and glue the plinth together.

8 Position assembled plinth onto the base (Fig 6). Mark its position and drill two fixing holes per wall. Screw plinth in position but do not glue.

9 Remove plinth from the base. This is to simplify the fitting of baize later.

10 Screw and glue the walls to the base.

11 Cut to size the storage compartment lid (Fig 19) and place it in position (see

Fig 6 Base
6 (¼) thick

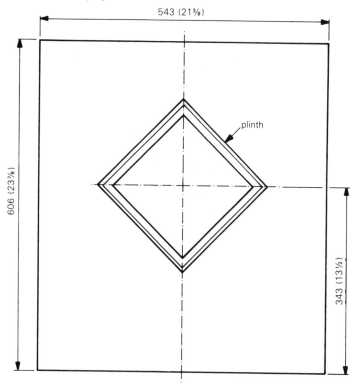

Fig 7 Plinth walls
make four

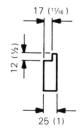

Fig 1). Mark hinge positions then proceed as step 3.

12 Screw and glue pole support block (Fig 9) in position (see Fig 1).

13 Cut pole to length (see Cutting List).

14 The light chain used to connect the swinging ball to the pole is the type which resembles lots of ball bearings joined together. It can be obtained from any good ironmonger's. Connecting the chain to the ball and pole uses standard connectors which must be bought with the chain.

15 Ideally the chain should be attached to the top of the pole by a swivel bearing, but

159

Fig 8 Plinth top
12 (½) thick

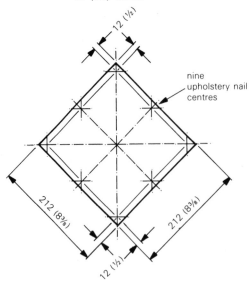

nine
upholstery nail
centres

12 (½)

212 (8⅜)

212 (8⅜)

12 (½)

Fig 9 Pole support block
70 (2¾) thick

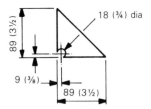

18 (¾) dia

89 (3½)

9 (⅜)

89 (3½)

pole — 1130 (44½) long x 18 (¾) dia

Fig 10 Storage compartment lid
16 (⅝) thick

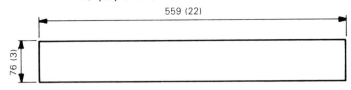

559 (22)

76 (3)

hinge positions — see Fig 1

Fig 11 Skittles
make nine

section on centre line

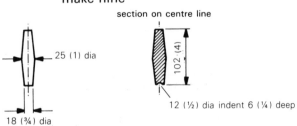

25 (1) dia

102 (4)

18 (¾) dia

12 (½) dia indent 6 (¼) deep

to reproduce this arrangement at home would require very specialised engineering equipment. A much simpler and quite satisfactory method of attaching the chain to the pole is as follows:

a) Connect one end of the chain (via a connector) to a hook. The type of hook required will be one which secures a bathroom sink plug to its chain, and is formed into two loops.

b) Insert a pan head screw into the smallest loop.

c) Place a flat washer between the loop and the pole, and screw the assembly into the top of the pole.

d) Do not over-tighten the screw, as free movement is essential.

e) Use a screwed eye via a connector to secure the chain to the swinging ball.

16 Cut to length the nine skittles (Fig 11), and drill a 12mm (½in) dia indent in the bottom of each one before shaping it.

17 Smooth off all faces and edges and varnish. Do not varnish the bottom 70mm (2¾in) of the pole which fits into the pole support block, or any surface which is going to be covered with contact adhesive when fitting the baize. Contact adhesives can be very good paint strippers and on contact with varnish will result in making an uneven surface underneath the baize.

18 Before varnishing the skittles, drill a small pilot hole in the bottom of each one and partially screw in a 25mm (1in) long round head screw. Wrap one end of a short length of wire around the screw and make a hook in the other end so that the varnished skittle can be hung up to dry.

19 When varnishing has been completed, spread contact adhesive evenly over baize areas. Working from one side, press baize firmly onto adhesive. Baize should be available from an upholsterer in a variety of colours, but as it is not a commonly used material it may have to be ordered.

20 Screw plinth in position and hammer upholstery nails in position (Fig 8). Protect the head of the nails with PVC tape.

Cutting list

Back wall (Fig 2)	1 off	559×76×25mm (22×3×1in)	Wood
Side walls (Fig 3)	2 off	622×76×25mm (24½×3×1in)	Wood
Inner wall (Fig 4)	1 off	533×70×25mm (21×2¾×1in)	Wood
Front wall (Fig 5)	1 off	559×60×25mm (22×2⅜×1in)	Wood
Base (Fig 6)	1 off	543×606×6mm (21⅜×23⅞×¼in)	Plywood
Plinth walls (Fig 7)	4 off	228×70×25mm (9×2¾×1in)	Wood
Plinth top (Fig 8)	1 off	212×212×12mm (8⅜×8⅜×½in)	Wood
Pole support block	1 off	89×89×70mm (3½×3½×2¾in)	Wood
Pole	1 off	1130mm (44½in) long×18mm (¾in) dia dowel	
Storage compartment lid (Fig 10)	1 off	559×76×16mm (22×3×⅝in)	Wood
Skittles	9 off	102mm (4in) long×25mm (1in) dia dowel	
Swinging ball	1 off	44mm (1¾in) dia	Wood

Ancillaries

Magnetic catch (Fig 5)	1 off	
Hinges (Fig 1)	2 off	51mm (2in) long
Baize (plinth)	1 off	228mm (9in) square
(walled area)	1 off	509×497mm (20×19½in)
(storage compartment)	1 off	171×629mm (6¾×24¾in)
Upholstery nails	9 off	
Light chain	1 off	996mm (39¼in) long
Chain connectors	2 off	
Screwed eye	1 off	

NURSERY MOBILE AND TEMPLATES

Young children are very interested in anything that moves, and babies who may spend a lot of time in their cot lying on their backs like to have something to focus their attention on.

This project will give you a long-lasting mobile of your choice, with the added advantage of being able to use its components as templates when the mobile is no longer required.

You can make as many or as few designs as required, and when one tem-

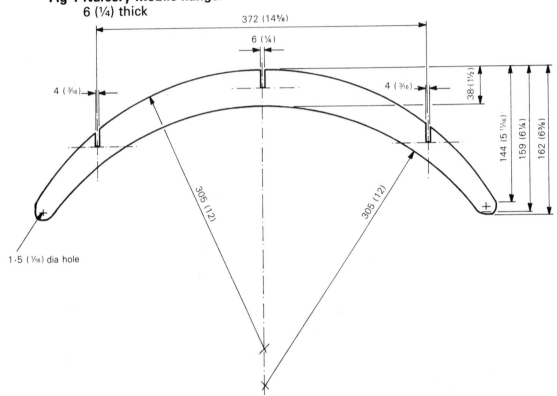

Fig 1 Nursery mobile hanger
6 (¼) thick

372 (14⅝)

6 (¼)

4 (3/16)

4 (3/16)

38 (1½)

144 (5 11/16)

159 (6¼)

162 (6⅜)

305 (12)

305 (12)

1·5 (1/16) dia hole

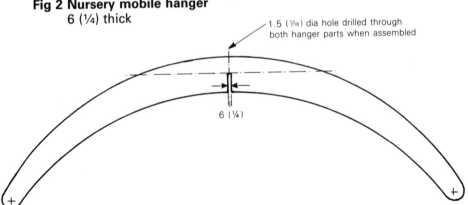

Fig 2 Nursery mobile hanger
6 (¼) thick

1.5 (1/16) dia hole drilled through both hanger parts when assembled

6 (¼)

plate has been made, it can easily be used to reproduce further templates of the same design. Your templates can either be left in a natural finish or painted in bright colours.

By using grids of various sizes, larger templates can be made (see colour photo page 25). It is important that only birch plywood is used throughout this project, as ordinary plywood will have ragged edges (see Methods and Materials page 8).

1 To enable the 305mm (12in) radii to be drawn (Figs 1 and 2), a compass will have to be made. Refer to Doll's Rocking Cradle, step 1 (page 16) for method of how to do this.

2 When the hangers have been cut out and assembled (no glue is needed in this project), drill a 1.5mm ($^{1/16}$in) dia hole, vertically through both of them where they intersect, through which a hanging cord can be threaded.

3 To transpose the template drawings onto your work piece, draw a grid of the size shown for each drawing onto a piece of tracing paper, and copy the required shape square by square.

4 To give maximum strength to your templates, the wood grain should follow the direction shown in each drawing.

5 Use fishing line to attach shapes to hanger.

Parrot
4 ($^{3/16}$) thick

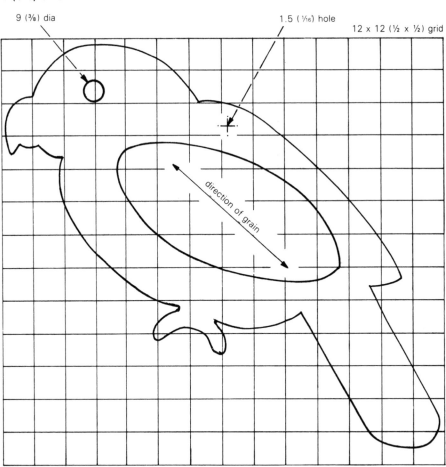

9 ($^{3/8}$) dia

1.5 ($^{1/16}$) hole

12 x 12 ($^{1/2}$ x $^{1/2}$) grid

direction of grain

Butterfly
4 (³⁄₁₆) thick

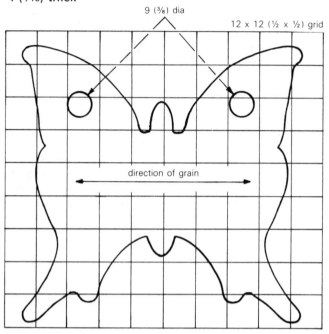

9 (³⁄₈) dia

12 x 12 (½ x ½) grid

direction of grain

Witch
4 (³⁄₁₆) thick

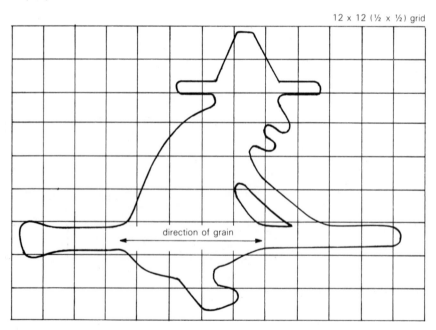

12 x 12 (½ x ½) grid

direction of grain

164

Horse
4 (³⁄₁₆) thick

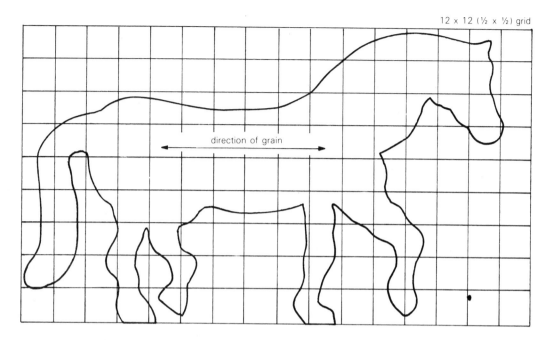

12 x 12 (½ x ½) grid

direction of grain

Microbus
4 (³⁄₁₆) thick

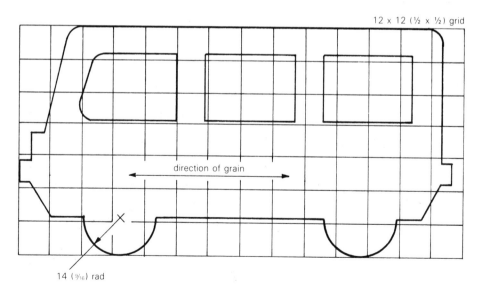

12 x 12 (½ x ½) grid

direction of grain

14 (⁹⁄₁₆) rad

Helicopter
4 (³⁄₁₆) thick

12 x 12 (½ x ½) grid

direction of grain

Ship
4 (³⁄₁₆) thick

12 x 12 (½ x ½) grid

direction of grain

Dinosaur
4 (³⁄₁₆) thick

direction of grain

12 x 12 (½ x ½) grid

Man in the moon
4 (³⁄₁₆) thick

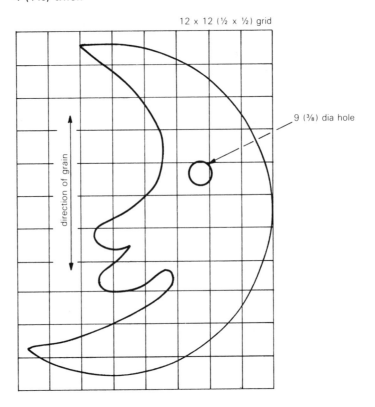

12 x 12 (½ x ½) grid

direction of grain

9 (³⁄₈) dia hole

Car
4 (³⁄₁₆) thick

12 x 12 (½ x ½) grid

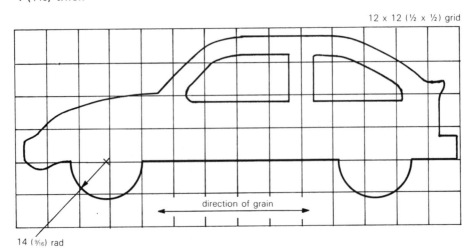

direction of grain

14 (⁹⁄₁₆) rad

Van
4 (³⁄₁₆) thick

12 x 12 (½ x ½) grid

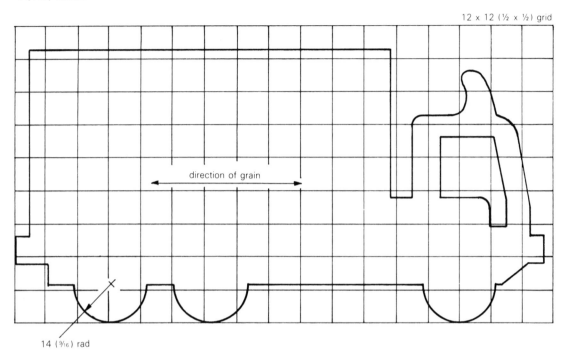

direction of grain

14 (⁹⁄₁₆) rad

ACKNOWLEDGEMENTS

I would like to acknowledge the following people and companies for their help in putting together *Making Wooden Toys For All Ages*:

Mr P. L. Harrison, Marketing Services Manager, Alvis Ltd, for providing material for the Stalwart Amphibious Lorry; Mr M. Steels SIO DPR(A), Ministry of Defence Directorate of Public Relations (Army), who allowed the Stalwart Amphibious Truck to be used as a project; Susan Pownall, Marketing Co-ordinator, Corgi Toys Ltd, for providing the die-cast models for the Rescue Centre; Peter Byrne, Matchbox Toys Ltd, who supplied the US police cars and Snorkel fire engine model used in the photograph of the Rescue Centre; Mr A. R. Norton, Deputy Managing Director, Copyright Promotions Ltd, for use of the 'Starcom' models in the photograph Space Port Nasus 5; Paul McGarry, Product Group Manager Coleco UK Inc, for providing the 'Starcom' models in the photograph of Space Port Nasus 5; Karen Jiggens, Stocksigns Ltd, and Tony Mawby, Signs & Labels Ltd, for signs used on the Rescue Centre and Space Port Nasus 5; Sandra L. Stas, Public Relations Administrator, Volvo GM Heavy Truck Corporation, for providing information towards the construction of Spirit of America; Helen Davies, Black & Decker Ltd, for material used in the Power Tools section; Don Laughton for kindly loaning the Max Zaph dolls in the colour photographs; my wife Susan for making the seat for the Doll's Buggy; Pam Griffiths, my hard-working editor at David & Charles for her work in editing and putting the finishing touches to this book; the staff of my local library (Barry) for their assistance in researching the Table Skittles game (Devil Among the Tailors).

INDEX

Photographs are indicated in *italic* type.